Acknowledgments

Special thanks go to Elissa Summerfield for her expertise and discerning counsel in editing the manuscript. I greatly appreciate the help of Dr. Lucille Zeph, Debbie Gilmer, Sue Russell, Alan Parks, and Kerrilyn Porro from The University of Maine Center for Community Inclusion in bringing this book to fruition. Their dedication to people with disabilities in Maine is truly inspiring. I am indebted to my University of Minnesota Ph.D. advisor and scholar Dr. John Rynders who fundamentally influenced my understanding of Down syndrome and developmental disabilities.

Gratitude is extended to Dixie Leavitt, Ms. BJ Barton, and Carolyn Merchant for sharing their recollections of Paige Barton. Kelly Klymer and Peter Stowell were helpful in providing feedback on the early drafts of the manuscript. I am especially grateful to Dennis Strout for his generosity in conducting the consumer advocate interviews, and to Arthur Lerman of Support Solutions and Port Resources, agencies supporting the self-advocacy effort in Maine. Pat Farmer, Steve Cantrell, Dr. John Cary, Barb Van Herreweghe, and others were extremely gracious in sharing memories of Paige, precious photos, and stories of her involvement with the Support Organization for Trisomy 18, 13, and Related Disorders. I commend Maine Representative Randall L. Berry as Sponsor of the Legislative Sentiment displayed on the plaque mentioned in Governor King's forward to this book.

During this project my husband David and my sons Aaron and Ian vicariously experienced the story of Paige's life through our many probing and memorable discussions. They were always willing to listen, read, and respond with wisdom and honesty, never tiring of this lengthy endeavor.

As I gathered the material for this book, I was privileged to encounter many people who revealed new dimensions of Paige's work and personality. Unfortunately, it was not possible to include all the events and people touched by Paige. The incidents in this book are recorded as Paige and others remembered them. They were subjectively interpreted and translated, reflecting personal perspectives and biases.

Most important are Paige's many friends, the self-advocates she loved and served. I urge them to carry forward with Paige's worthy goals of independence, choice, and self-determination.

Beyond All Expectations

The Story of Paige Barton

by
JoAnne Putnam, Ph.D.

Published by The University of Maine
            Center for Community Inclusion
            5717 Corbett Hall
            Orono, ME 04469 - 5717
            (207) 581 - 1084 (V/TTY)

Library of Congress Control Number: 2003103613

Cover and interior design by Kerrilyn Porro

Printed by Cushing-Malloy in Ann Arbor, Michigan

Books and articles quoted or cited in the text under the usual fair use allowances are acknowledged in the references.

To my best friend and sister,
Mary McNab

Foreword

As governor of the State of Maine, it is with great fondness and respect that I contribute these notes to the important story of Paige Barton. Paige received her B.S. at the University of Maine at Farmington, which eventually led to her employment as a Consumer Advocate with the Maine Department of Behavior and Developmental Services. And what an advocate she was!

Leadership within the complexity of State Government requires many things: energy, commitment, clarity of vision and much hard work. Paige excelled at all of these, from building a unified self-advocacy movement for people with developmental disabilities, to presenting herself and her clear mission at every opportunity, to laughing and crying at the difficulty of the tasks ahead. Paige's life and her work were strengthened by her years in institutions - rather than being embittered by those years, she developed the commitment to battle the injustices that are endured by too many. The Maine Legislature passed a legislative sentiment in her honor, and a plaque, which is displayed in the departmental offices, summarizes her work and spirit in this way:

"Through her mentoring, support, and encouragement of people with disabilities, Paige helped people focus on their 'abilities' and through her tenacity, sense of humor, and fun loving spirit, advocated for others and helped them to 'Speak Up For Themselves'."

Paige touched many lives and is sorely missed. Her life's work and vision lives on reminding us all to keep at the struggle to live up to our true capacities and never to give up on our dreams.

Respectfully,

Angus S. King, Jr.
Governor, State of Maine
1995 - 2002

Introduction

*The way a society views and responds to disability and
people with disabilities says as much about the society as
it does about disability. American society has changed in
some fundamental and dramatic ways since the 1950's and
so have notions of what is acceptable, what is valued, and
who belongs.*

D. Hagner

It was an honor to be asked to write this foreword. Paige's
life and her story, as told here by her dear friend and colleague Dr.
JoAnne Putnam, truly embody the spirit, intent and desires of all we
do and seek to do at The University of Maine Center for Community
Inclusion, Maine's University Center for Excellence in Developmental
Disabilities Education, Research and Service.

As we celebrate our tenth anniversary in 2002 it is most
appropriate to include the publication of Paige's book as one of
our celebratory year activities. Paige was an original member of our
Consumer Advisory Committee and therefore played an integral role
in shaping the Center's mission, purpose and early initiatives. One of
those early efforts was to support the development of a statewide self
advocacy organization for individuals with developmental disabilities.
Paige was intimately involved in this project and provided leadership,
mentoring and support to many individuals across the state who were
inspired by her accomplishments and all she brought to her work.
Speaking Up For Us of Maine continues to be guided by Paige's vision
and passion.

While JoAnne's poignant tale of Paige's life is unfolded on the
following pages, I wish I could report that the opportunities and rich

life that Paige crafted for herself reflected the opportunities and life stories of all individuals in our state and nation with developmental disabilities. Today children and adults with developmental disabilities continue to lead lives too typically characterized by segregation, poverty, and loneliness that characterized much of Paige's life. With limited choice regarding where and with whom to live, a lack of control over both human and fiscal resources, realizing the dreams and desires that Paige held for herself unfortunately remains out of reach for hundreds and thousands of individuals and their families.

Federal and state initiatives have been numerous and lives have improved over the years, of that there is no doubt. Efforts continue to carve out reform and renewal efforts in our schools to assure that all students have access to a high quality and meaningful education that leads to meaningful and valued lives and careers in the community of one's choice. Reform of long-term care systems, especially self determination initiatives and systems change projects, is demonstrating that living valued and meaningful lives in inclusive communities is not only possible, but life enhancing. Real jobs, meaningful careers and self employment have allowed individuals to enjoy valued lives with increased self sufficiency, economic power, and have demonstrated that segregated work activity centers and sheltered employment don't need to be a part of our "continuum" of services.

Debbie Gilmer
Coordinator of Community Services
The University of Maine Center for Community Inclusion

Table of Contents

Chapter 1

Shooting Star

Perhaps they are not the stars,
but rather openings in Heaven
where the love of our lost ones
pours through and shines down upon us
to let us know they are happy.

-Inspired by an Eskimo Legend

Physically weary and emotionally drained by the four-hour drive from the hospital in Waterville, Maine, I finally made it to our northern Maine homestead after dark. It was Tuesday, August 24, 1999. Winding up Hilltop Road past the Belgian draft horses quietly grazing in the upper pasture, I parked my car and walked slowly and unsteadily across the lawn to the dooryard. My path was lit by the moon and brilliant stars. I was struck by the splendor of the northern sky adorned with heavenly lights. Yet the celestial beauty of the night only deepened the sadness I felt knowing my dying friend could not share the experience.

Throwing my L.L. Bean satchel on the pine floor in its accustomed place, I called for my husband David and my youngest son Ian to discuss the doleful, unexpected turn of events. What started out as a routine monthly drive to Augusta for an advisory board meeting had turned tragic.

For a while, I sat quietly in a chair on the front deck, reflecting on the enormity of what had befallen my dear friend at the hospital. The moon backlit the spruce and fir spires, illuminating Lone Bear Ridge across the valley. The fields twinkled with fireflies and a barred owl repeated its "who hoots for you" call from the cedar swamp.

By chance we were both watching the same quadrant of southern sky, as a falling star blazed across, leaving its ghost of a trail. With my family surrounding me, I tried to recount my agonizing visit to the hospital.

Just as I began to speak, the phone interrupted. It was Dixie Leavitt, Paige's accessibility assistant and driver, who confirmed what I knew was imminent...Paige Barton had died. While Dixie and I talked, our three dogs began to howl mournfully into the night. Their baying, which continued through most of the phone conversation, was mystifying. I shivered, knowing that something inexplicable had just unfolded. Even my scientifically minded archaeologist husband, David, reacted with wonder at the dogs' sorrowful cries.

After hanging up, I returned to the deck. Dropping into the chair, I blurted without preamble to David that I had finally mustered the courage to visit Paige.

A week earlier, after learning that Paige had been admitted to hospital, I phoned the waiting room asking for Paige's mother. Ms. Barton gave me a briefing on Paige's medical condition, and I asked her if I might visit the hospital to see Paige. She told me without explanation that a visit wasn't a good idea. I said I understood and asked Ms. Barton to call me, please, with any updates on Paige's medical status and to let me know when I could see her.

I had every intention of driving to Waterville to see Paige at a moment's notice, and had already made arrangements with the President of the University of Maine at Presque Isle, informing her that I might take some personal days from my dean's position to visit my seriously ill friend. President Hensel was sympathetic, as I had confided in her about Paige's tenuous hold on life, and she knew of Paige's significance to me.

Anxiously awaiting a call for almost a week I assumed that no news was good news. I felt conflicted about going to see her. On one hand, I wanted to honor her mother's wishes; on the other hand, I knew that Paige would have wanted me to come.

Maine's Moxie Lady

On the morning of my four and a half-hour drive south to Augusta, there was ample time to reflect. Engrossed in my thoughts, I lost the first fifty miles on Route 1, oblivious to the pastoral landscape of lush potato fields framed by vistas of woodland and mountains, horizons so distant and space so expansive, they seemed to be an eastern counterpart to North Dakota. But I didn't notice. I couldn't stop thinking about Paige; I needed to see her.

On Interstate 95 fifteen miles south of Houlton, the north face of Katahdin, the sacred mountain of the Wabanaki, rose dramatically above all else. Seeing the dawn sun glisten on the peaks, glinting on a splotch of residual snow above the massive cirque, infused me with energy and resolve. The view conjured up the exhilaration and confidence I feel when climbing Baxter Peak, negotiating gingerly across the perilous ridge of the Knife Edge. I yearned to be up there at that moment, illuminated by the first rays of the sun while the surrounding land and all of its denizens lay cloaked in darkness below. At that moment, I felt as if I had sweated and scrambled to a heightened state of perception, which never fails to restore the soul.

It came to me that I was losing my spirit, like many busy professionals, in the busy people-pleasing work-a-day world. I had lost my way, been symbolically lured from the path to wander aimlessly in the dark forest. Was Paige ever deterred from pursuing her goals by a lack of a formal invitation? What would she wish me to do? Why was I actually worrying about whether I should visit Paige because I didn't have an invitation from her family?

By the time I crossed the Penobscot River, the confluence of the East and West Branches forming the great arterial flow that is the life-blood of Maine, my ambiguity had fled with the vanished darkness. I was going to see Paige to attempt to revive her life blood...and mine.

Crossing Birch Stream, where the Penobscot people paddle in search of basket wood, the highway enters and bisects Alton Bog. Next to Katahdin, it's my favorite landmark on the drive from north to south.

Most visitors to Maine travelling north beyond Bangor are surprised to leave the comfort of a landscape replete with familiar components of their own homes and to drop suddenly into the sprawling sub-arctic. Few are even aware of the bog, only vaguely sensing that they have entered a marsh. Indeed, the term "bog" likely elicits a shudder and visions of black muck, biting insects, and perceived but ill-defined horrors out of Poe's "The Fall of the House of Usher." But you can't begin to appreciate the wonder and beauty of these special places simply by gazing out the car window at a curiosity that flashes by at a mile a minute.

The bog is a vital, living thing...shunned by many, a wasteland scene indifferent to others, and cherished for its unique complexity and resilience by a prescient few. Tiny, brilliant red sundews spread their traps for insects, russet pitcher plants rest patiently in the sun for the unwary fly. White tufts of Arctic cotton grass bob in the August breeze. A teeming life that is bathed in dark red brown tannic acid bog water called Moxie. Then, later in the summer, it is desiccated and drought ridden. Frozen solid in winter and sustained only by the moist air of spring, the bog is nature's crowning achievement. It is life with all its vicissitudes, including death.

I adore the stunted, nutrient starved larch and black spruce that sprout surreally from hummocks of sphagnum moss. Their gnarled posture presents a beauty very different from their stately, well nourished brethren of the forest. It is a beauty of substance, unexpected age, and endurance, tempered by adversity in the harshest of situations. Those trees are Paige, I thought. Like them, she was dismissed early on by those seeking conformity, overlooked by a society oblivious to the uncommon. Her life was shaped by hardship as she turned adversity into crowning achievements. Her beauty was of substance. I smiled as a play of words on the song Foxy Lady entered my thoughts - Paige was a Moxie Lady!

Now determined to go the hospital in the afternoon, I thought what or whom would it hurt? I could be unobtrusive, and I wouldn't stay too long. Staunchly resolute, I stopped my ruminating.

Later that afternoon, after my meeting in Augusta, I headed to Waterville and found my way to The Thayer Unit, a fairly large teaching hospital with many floors and wings. A bit at a loss, I had to ask several people for directions to the right building and how to get to the 2nd floor Critical Care Unit (CCU).

It gave me the creeps, that feel of institution... I could smell the disinfectants and was repulsed by the latent memories of prior visits to institutions they stimulated. Paige would hate being held captive there, even if confinement were essential to her recovery.

When I entered the waiting room, I saw Paige's mother and eldest sister. It occurred to me that I had never met Ms. Barton face-to-face, although I'd spoken to her over the years and had seen her in Paige's videos. In person, she exudes a commanding, even imperious presence, despite her rather small stature. She appeared to be in her late seventies, with iron gray hair and wide-rimmed glasses. I detected a slight resemblance between Paige and her mom.

I felt a chill in the room despite the oppressive heat outside. Dixie was the first to approach me. What a welcome relief to see her rosy face, warm smile, and strawberry blonde hair that framed her head like the halo of an angel! She embraced me, but then her look turned serious. Escorting me to a corner of the waiting room, she said, in a gentle voice with a thick Maine accent lowered to a whisper, "JoAnne, in a few hours, Paige's life support will be removed. Paige's family has decided that it's futile to continue life support because her pneumonia isn't responding to antibiotics."

Thank God, I had followed my morning intuition to see Paige. As fate would have it, this was to be the last day of her life. I know it was beyond mere coincidence that I was at the hospital that afternoon.

The doctor had told Dixie that Paige had contracted a vicious fungal pneumonia over two weeks ago that was devastating her organ systems. Dixie recounted the prelude to Paige's hospitalization. The pair had attended a SOFT (Support Organization for Trisomy 18, 13 and Related Disorders) conference in Rochester, New York, the last week of July. The following week was a vacation week. On the weekend, Dixie invited Paige to go to Fun Town in Saco along with Dixie's husband, Ted, and their two grandchildren. Dixie knew something was amiss when Paige declined some of the rides. "She just wasn't herself," said Dixie. "When we went to McDonald's afterwards, Paige couldn't keep her food down. I thought she had a stomach flu."

On the drive home from Fun Town, Dixie asked Paige "Why didn't you tell me you were sick when I picked you up this morning?" Paige's reply was, "If I had told you, you wouldn't have taken me to Fun Town!" Paige's playful, childlike desires sometimes clouded her good judgment.

Dixie wondered if Paige had contracted the fungal pneumonia in the Jacuzzi at the Rochester conference, but the doctor said it was unlikely. When she saw Paige at church on Sunday, she asked her about her health. She replied, "So so...I'm here..." gesturing by raising both palms up.

On Monday, Dixie called Paige's doctor and picked up some medicine for her upset stomach. What Dixie encountered that evening was very disturbing. Paige was shaking from the chills and couldn't keep food down. "Still, we thought she just had the flu," recalls Dixie.

Dixie phoned on Tuesday, and again on Wednesday. By Wednesday, Paige was almost too weak to speak. Dixie immediately rushed to her apartment and drove her to her physician's office, and then to the Maine General Medical Center in Augusta. The doctor, also surmising that she had a severe case of the flu, decided to admit her for blood tests.

Thursday morning at 5:00, Dixie received a distressing call from the hospital. "Paige has taken a turn for the worse," said the doctor. "Her kidneys are failing. She needs to be transferred immediately to the Thayer unit in Waterville for dialysis."

When Dixie arrived at the hospital they had just inserted a clear plastic tube, powered by a respirator, to assist Paige's breathing.

"Paige was awake and she looked at me with wide eyes. I told her that her brother Peter was on his way, and that upset her. She tried to tell me something but the tube prevented her from talking," said Dixie.

Dixie knew she needed to contact Paige's family right away. But Ms. Barton had recently moved, and Dixie didn't have her new phone number. She remembered that Paige's brother worked for the Farmington Police Department, so she called there and left a message. Obviously, he received the message because both he and Ms. Barton went to Maine General and followed Paige's ambulance to Waterville.

There, the doctors tried a variety of antibiotics, but even the most potent was ineffective. She had developed rashes all over her body.

Dixie and I huddled in the corner of the hospital waiting room as Dixie somberly conveyed Paige's fate. Because Paige had not responded to a decrease in sedatives and remained in a coma, they had little hope for her recovery. To ease the transition from life support, I was told that the doctors would inject her with drugs to prevent her from waking when the tube was removed.

My God, I thought, They can't contemplate this! It was shocking news given that the status report I received in Presque Isle was that she was improving. Not at all prepared for Dixie's pronouncement, I was consumed with a feeling of helplessness. How could they give up on her strong will to live? But, unlike her family members, I had not been in the hospital for almost two weeks and could not understand the exhausting series of difficult decisions.

Still, at the moment, I felt that I should do something. But what? I wondered. Should I plead? Should I use logic? Without much thought, I proclaimed to those in the waiting room that so called "terminal" people can make miraculous recoveries!

Paige's life force was incredibly strong, and I wanted to believe that she would make a miraculous comeback from this crisis. However, for that marvel to happen, she would need assertive advocacy. Experienced though I was in advocating successfully for my own family, it wasn't my family member near death in the Critical Care Unit.

The waiting room became more crowded as Paige's Pastor, his Associate

Pastor, and a friend and colleague of Paige's came in. Dixie introduced me to Paul Tabor, Training Coordinator for Mental Retardation Services, who entered the waiting room while the Pastor was conferring with the family. Paul and I stepped into the hallway and reminisced about Paige's work and notable contributions to the disability field in Maine. At Dixie's urging, Paige's sister asked me to assist in writing Paige's obituary for the *Kennebec Journal.*

I wondered if my complicity in writing an obituary was a betrayal of Paige, who was still alive in a room not far away. The obituary made the finality of the decision to remove the life support more certain. Weighing the pros and cons, I decided to help because I was probably familiar with some of her achievements that others were not. Dixie, Paige's sister, and I sat at the round table in the waiting room after Ms. Barton went to lunch and compiled a list of Paige's accomplishments.

As we finished our work on the obituary, Paige's sister acknowledged Paige's impact in Maine and the nation. She said that Paige's life and work were "truly remarkable." I savored these words, wishing that Paige could hear her sister's tribute.

Before I could ask, Dixie informed me that the family did not want me to visit Paige's room. Later, I regretted not being able to say good bye. My son, Ian, who had known Paige since he was a baby, admonished me. "Why didn't you just sneak into her room to say good bye and then leave?" Children have a refreshing way of cutting through adult complexities.

"You're right, Ian," I told him. "If I had Paige's moxie, I would have boldly walked into her room, regardless of the consequences." Ian knew what Moxie was - it's a soft drink produced in Maine - and I knew what the word moxie meant - substance, courage and audacity. But for some reason I acquiesced, respecting her mother's wish in my typically compliant manner.

At about 3 o'clock I decided I should leave the hospital. I had a long drive home and I didn't want to be there when they disconnected my friend and protegé's life support. It was not a time for visitors outside the family.

Sensing my despair as we quietly bid our good-byes in the waiting room, Dixie suggested that I join her in a prayer for Paige. She then asked the Pastor to lead us in a group prayer. Dixie asked those in the room to hold hands and form a circle as we prayed for Paige's ultimate journey. We all stood up and clasped hands. As the Pastor began the prayer, my eyes closed and my throat swelled with sadness as I held back my tears.

Driving north on I-95, I pressed the radio scanner looking for the National Public Radio station. The scanner happened to stop at a station that was playing the old gospel tune "I'll Fly Away." The song, one of Paige's favorites, was playing at about the time she died. I can still hear the comforting words, "To my home on God's celestial shore, I'll fly away."

How I wished my friend would not go gently into that good night. Racing through my mind, tormented by sorrow, were fragments and questions. "Why now? Why not later? If only after a year, or just six months, why hadn't I bargained for Paige's life on earth with whatever fates may be?"

Why did I continue to question what others saw as the inevitable outcome of Paige's condition? As if they were mind readers, they assumed that she would have been miserable living in an extended care facility or on dialysis. During Paige's last day of consciousness, Dixie had asked her if she would want to live hooked up to a respirator. Her answer had been an emphatic "NO!"

Unfortunately, Paige had not legally indicated her wishes about life sustaining medical treatment when there was time for thoughtful reflection. Nor had she designated a health care proxy to make such decisions on her behalf should she slip into unconsciousness. Sadly, the Living Will papers were in Dixie's hands the night Paige was admitted to Maine General, when she was still conscious. Dixie fully intended to have Paige sign them but the nurse told her that Paige was too sick that evening, suggesting that it be done tomorrow...but tomorrow was too late.

Death came too soon. She had so much more she must accomplish. She was intent upon establishing Paige's Place, a home where people who did not possess the requisites for independent living could live and learn what they needed, and ultimately reside on their own. Her plan was to hire people who would come into her home while she was at work and teach three or four roommates how to cook and clean, along with other essential domestic skills. After about six months of training, her temporary roommates would move into their own homes. Paige's Place would become an authentic, vibrant classroom for autonomous living. She had been exploring these possibilities by attending classes on how to obtain a FHA loan and how to purchase a home for her project.

Chapter 2

Requiem for a Heroine

If only I could so live and so serve the world that after
me there should never again be birds in cages . . .
-Isak Dinesen

As Ian and I drove to Chelsea on August 27th, the day of Paige's funeral, the roadsides were lined with goldenrod and cerulean blue chicory. The air was humid and flocks of evening grosbeaks swarmed carelessly along the highways, oblivious of the traffic. Iridescent teal and blue dragonflies, bumblebees, and monarch butterflies were everywhere that summer - a Maine summer as sunny and dry as I could remember. The heat was oppressive - hot enough to threaten the health of the elderly and infirm, according to news reports.

The Kennebec Valley Assembly of God Church is in the town of Chelsea, not far from Augusta, the state capital. To get on the road to Chelsea in Augusta, we needed to negotiate two roundabouts. The first was near the capitol building, leading to the road that crosses the Memorial Bridge over the Kennebec River. Crossing the bridge, I remembered when the road crews constructed the mesh fences on the sides of the bridge to prevent pedestrians from jumping to their deaths. I heard it was after a rash of suicides by former Augusta Mental Health Institute (AMHI) residents who, caught by overzealous attempts to implement deinstitutionalization, had been released into the community without proper support. A second roundabout beyond the bridge led to the Stone Street exit.

Traveling east on Stone Street past the neatly painted wood frame houses, I passed the Augusta Mental Health Institute on the right. Seeing AMHI always makes me shudder. A foreboding cluster of red brick buildings comprise the compound. It resembles a prison, complete with iron bars on the windows to prevent escape. The beautiful grounds with stately maples and green lawns belie a shameful history of tortured lives and punitive methods.

Paige had been employed by the Office of Consumer Affairs in the Maine Department of Mental Health, Mental Retardation and Substance Abuse. Recently her office had been relocated from the State Office Building near the capitol to new quarters in the Marquardt Building, a vacated institutional residence hall at AMHI. It was a move she made with great trepidation.

Paige had been tormented by recurring nightmares of being locked away in an institution. I was amazed that she managed to adjust to a new office in this haunting institutional setting. Although her life's goal was to see these horrific monoliths closed, she seemed unable to escape them herself. Fortunately, she spent most of her work time traveling, so she was rarely there. Dixie said she never really adjusted to the AMHI office building, often crying when she was there.

We reached the Assembly of God Church, a humble white structure with a small steeple and a single cross identifying its religious usage. I hoped it would be large enough to accommodate the crowd gathering to pay their last respects.

It was only three days since her death, so many of the people who knew her were not yet aware of her passing. Others who lived farther away, or who were on their summer vacations, would not be able to make the service. Consequently, arrangements were already being made by colleagues at work to host another service in the fall, designed to be a celebration of her life.

First to arrive at the church were members of her family: four sisters, two brothers, nieces, an aunt, and her mother. They carried themselves with an air of poise and dignity characteristic of well-educated, refined New Englanders. Next a mixture of professionals from the disability and human services fields had disembarked from a van. Along with them came a small number of their constituents, "consumers" of disability, mental health, and mental retardation services. Their attire was more humble, but respectable. The relative casualness of their garments, compared to those of the Bartons, hinted at social distinctions and a diversity among those in attendance. People who knew one another stood in the parking lot and quietly conversed. Soon the lot filled with vehicles as it neared time for the service to begin at 11:00 a.m.

The inside of the church was softly lit, casting a sacred hue in the sanctuary. Noticeable was the drum set in the chancel, evidence of the Assembly of God sect's spirited religious services. Somehow, I thought, the drums were expressive of Paige's high-spiritedness. In the front was an attractive woman in a sleek black dress. She would be the sign language interpreter for the ceremony.

Dixie was the usher. She seated us in a pew near the front. As I looked around, I recognized many of Paige's friends. Most important were the people with disabilities, or "self-advocates," as Paige referred to them. There were also colleagues and key figures from state government, the university, and disability advocacy organizations. Looking down the pew to my left I was amazed to see the former and acting Maine State Commissioners of Mental Health, Mental Retardation and Substance Abuse; the Director of the Division of Mental Retardation; the Director of the Office of Consumer Affairs; and the Executive Director of OHI, a local agency that provides supports to people with disabilities in the community. Behind me was the Director of the Maine State Developmental Disabilities Council and the Acting Director of the Center for Community Inclusion. Paige would have been honored to know that so many associates and friends were there. Friends and family journeyed from great distances, driving hundreds of miles or flying from as far away as Ohio, Pennsylvania, and Texas. The enormous irony was that up until 11 years before, Paige was a pariah, deemed retarded and incapable of socialization, relegated to segregated institutions for people with mental retardation. But at her death she was a luminary who attracted a heterogeneous amalgam of mourners.

Seated in the left front pew were members of the Barton family. Their comportment was reverent yet reserved. Also in attendance were fellow church members and people associated with disability advocacy organizations. All told, about 275 people from all walks of life came to say goodbye. The turnout squeezed into the church was quite remarkable.

I suspect that almost everyone at the funeral knew that Paige had spent almost 15 years living in institutions for people with mental retardation. Many of the visitors crowded into the church understood well enough what warehousing people meant, even if they did not know the unhappy details of Paige's time in institutions. Though confronted by unspeakable adversity, Paige, undaunted, heroically defeated the odds by living longer than anyone with her disorder, by earning a college de-

gree, and more: independence, a job, a voice...in short, notable personhood. Her legacy will ripple through the lives of innumerable people
with and without disabilities for years to come.

For thirteen years, I had watched my friend blossom, and now I grieved
over the tragedy of a bloom picked prematurely - a life cut short while
nearing the height of professional and personal momentum. Paige
created her own brand of carpe diem philosophy. With tremendous
vitality and dedication, she had managed to escape institutionalization,
educate herself, and pack into one decade what it takes most people
two or even three decades to accomplish. She was reaching her dream
of contributing to the betterment of the lives of people with disabilities. I mourned because I would miss profoundly the inspiration of her
indomitable spirit, in sum, her passion for life.

Others at the funeral might have reasoned that, given her disorder,
Paige was lucky to live as long as she did and to achieve as much as she
had. Dixie had alluded to the toll her failing health was taking on her
ability to function in her work. Even journalists' tributes in the *Bangor
Daily News* ascribed her demise to the medical complications associated
with her "genetic anomaly." Columnist Tom Weber wrote that Paige's
legacy "scintillates compassion" and insightfully added that Paige was
"tough, resilient, and funny. She didn't ask for sympathy and tears."
But the sympathetic Weber accepted her death without protest.

Sitting next to me at the funeral was Bonnie Brooks, the Executive Director of OHI. I first met Bonnie in the airport in Anchorage, Alaska,
when she and Paige attended the "People First" conference in 1994.
At the time I was a professor at the University of Alaska Anchorage.
Astonishingly, Paige fulfilled her promise to visit me in Alaska someday.

Bonnie was quoted in the *Bangor Daily* as saying that on the night that Paige died, "I went out and looked at the stars. As I watched them twinkle and blink out, I thought of Paige and felt that a bright light had gone from the world."

Reverend Brad Pucket's words were profound. "It's not surprising that a person who brought such joy, hope and love by her life would bring such sorrow by her death." He said that "What Paige was in public was largely due to what she was in private. Her boldness, courage, and strength found its impetus in her faith in Jesus Christ."

I fantasized about Paige's unfulfilled dreams during the funeral, allowing my gaze to wander to her portrait that rested on a lace doily on the church's communion table in front of the podium. Paige was very proud of this picture of her and former First Lady Barbara Bush. Near the picture frame was a profusion of miniature white roses and a gorgeous bouquet of peach roses from one of her sisters. Because Paige was cremated, there was no coffin. My mind imagined, "We could still work together - even if she were on dialysis, even if she were reduced to living on a respirator." I simply could not accept that she was gone.

Perhaps it was selfish - even retributive - that the only comforting thought I had was that Paige had proven her case. She had demonstrated how she and all people pigeonholed as disabled, and thus useless burdens to society, represented so much more than their designated deviant status implied. Indeed, she stunned her family, her institutional caregivers, her friends, and the nation in exceeding by far the expectations of the various medical and educational labels assigned to her over the course of a lifetime. She proved that she was not simply a "mongoloid," or "mentally retarded."

Her life had been a constant struggle against physical pain. But the type of pain she endured from societal rejection caused by the misconceptions about her condition was much more hurtful. Who was this person underneath the label? How had she managed to achieve such professional success, such high regard in the community? What were the circumstances and personal qualities that encouraged her to move forward, to maneuver around all the barriers imposed by society and family?

She asked me to share her story for two reasons. First, she never wanted anyone else to have to endure the nightmarish experiences that she had encountered in her own life. No one, she felt, should have to suffer the condescension, rebuffs, and abandonment she encountered when dispatched to institutions and segregated facilities. Her dream was for all people with disabilities to enjoy an opportunity to contribute to society through productive work and community involvement. Second, she said she wanted people to "see beyond the label" - to get to know and understand the multidimensional aspects of the individual behind the "disability" appellation. Her life had been shaped in large part by assumptions and expectations about a presumed disability that was largely misconstrued. She also knew that many other people were circumscribed by their labels, whether because of a disability, poverty, sexual orientation, or racial background.

Paige and I started gathering material for this book in 1988. Barriers of physical distance, professional obligations, family obligations, and, frankly, my own ambitions intervened and slowed our writing progress. It wasn't until we visited Apple Creek State Mental Hospital in 1997 that I decided we had the proper documentation to back up her shocking claims of institutional mistreatment. Fortunately, the time that elapsed over these years permitted many conversations, trips, and professional activities, through which I gained a deepening appreciation of and love for my friend. At times, Paige's approach to dealing with adversity seemed enlightened and sanguine. Her ability to forgive others and her optimistic outlook were almost sage-like. She also had a plucky side that radiated a "don't mess with me" attitude. Her childlike humor was refreshing, her laughter, contagious. But she was human, and she succumbed, as most do, to life's temptations and self-destructive behaviors.

Reflecting on my deep connection with Paige, I realized that we lived parallel lives. Beginning in adolescence, we both participated in the historical drama of institutionalization, deinstitutionalization, and community inclusion of people with disabilities. Our vantage points differed, because we operated from diametrically opposite sides of the bolted institutional doors. However, our subjective perspectives on the horrors of institutions and the devastating effects of societal rejection were strikingly similar. Independently, we had come to find meaning and purpose in our lives through education and careers in the disability field, both determined to improve the quality of life of society's most marginalized people. Fortuitously and nearly impossibly, in the 1980's our parallel paths would intersect at a very important juncture for both of us: the university.

Chapter 3

The University of Maine at Farmington

We began by imagining that we are giving to them;
we end by realizing that they have enriched us.
-Pope John Paul II

It was late November in 1986. The sky was steely gray, and a blustery wind stirred the damp brown maple leaves bordering the sidewalk. Snowflakes were beginning to fall as students and professors scurried to and from their classes. Climbing the hill, I rehashed the lecture I had just delivered. My confidence in my teaching ability was sagging, but I still was doggedly determined to become a competent, if not outstanding, university professor. Mulling over what to me was my somewhat pedestrian presentation, I was about halfway up the hill to my office building, a stately brick edifice replete with English ivy, arched entrances, and a bell tower. A small, regional campus, the University of Maine at Farmington served 2,000 students pursuing undergraduate degrees in liberal arts, education, and human services. U.S. News and World Report ranked it as one of the top ten buys for a liberal arts education.

Located in Farmington, a town of about 7,400, the grounds were neatly maintained. Students and faculty enjoyed walking beneath the magnificent white pines in the campus park and across the arched bridge, or sitting on a park bench by the pond - even as the bitterly cold Maine winter chilled the air.

Twenty minutes out of town were the rolling mountains of western Maine, fragrant with balsam fir and covered with blueberries in late summer. It was a great area for cross-country skiing, biking, and hiking. The campus itself wasn't nearly as attractive or as noted as that of Bates or Bowdoin Colleges, or as large as The University of Maine System flagship campus in Orono, but I was more than satisfied with having landed my first faculty position at this close-knit, welcoming undergraduate institution.

Actually, I was surprised at how well I seemed to fit into this university community. Since I had lived on the fringes of society in the past, it was hard for my family and friends to envision me working in such a traditional institution. My last two years of undergraduate school at Colorado State University in the late sixties were turbulent - torn by the sometimes furious Vietnam antiwar protests. While not directly involved in violent protests, I questioned the war and sought refuge from the dominant establishment by living "off the land" in a commune in Virginia and in the Appalachian Mountains of West Virginia until the late seventies.

While residing at the Skyfields communal farm in the Shenandoah Mountains of Virginia, I found rewarding work at the "National Children's Rehabilitation Center," a residential school for children with epilepsy. What perplexed me was why these bright, normally functioning children had been removed from their schools and communities to a residential school just because they happened to have epilepsy. But in the early seventies, epilepsy carried such an ugly stigma that concerned parents decided their children would be better off attending a special school where they were protected from societal scorn and where their epilepsy was understood and could be treated. At the time, medication to treat seizures had not fully evolved. Unable to receive any controlling pharmacology, many of the girls in my unit experienced severe, debilitating seizures that resulted in falls, serious injuries, and even unconsciousness. Without pharmaceutical interventions, early death was a real possibility for some of the students. I was shocked and saddened to learn that four of the students had died during seizures or from falls only a few years after their graduation from the Rehabilitation Center.

Working with children with disabilities turned out to be the most fulfilling job I'd held. It caused me to break my vow never to become a teacher, and I enrolled in the Master's of Special Education program at West Virginia University. Thus, I extricated myself from an emotionally draining and self-absorbed phase of my life to one in which I was suffused with a sense of purpose and self-abandonment. Further education plus a cause were exactly what I needed.

After about five rewarding years teaching special education in West Virginia, I went on to obtain my doctorate at the University of Minnesota. My next step was to seek a university position as a professor of teacher education at a small campus in a rural area perfectly suited to my interests in rural living and to my desire to work within a genial, open-hearted community.

The University of Minnesota's doctoral program in Educational Psychology had infused my work a sense of direction and passion. At that time, the mainstreaming and deinstitutionalization movements to include children and adults with disabilities in regular classrooms and community residences were in full swing. The faculty with whom I studied at the University were on the forefront of the national research and policy making on mainstreaming and community living. During my four years of study I assisted in research on adults with Down syndrome, deinstitutionalization of people with disabilities, and instructional strategies for mainstreaming and inclusion. My dissertation was on cooperative learning and inclusion. At the time, cooperative group learning was just becoming a popular, highly effective alternative to the competitive and individualist instructional approaches that had dominated American education for so many decades. My humble contribution was to show how cooperative group learning could be efficaciously employed with students with disabilities in regular classrooms.

These were truly exciting times in the special education and disability fields. Finally, the nation was beginning to recognize that the aims of the Civil Rights movement also applied to people with disabilities. Numerous court decisions and legislation enacted during the late sixties through the eighties upheld equal opportunity in education and ruled against segregation and discrimination. We were pushing American educators to consider the feasibility and importance of inclusive education for even the most severely disabled learners. We were challenging the notion that any student could be deemed ineducable. We were demonstrating through our research that all students can learn and develop, no matter how profound their disability.

Armed with a degree and hands-on experience, I now had the ammunition to assume the gigantic responsibility of preparing future teachers committed to making a difference in the lives of children historically marginalized by society and excluded from mainstream education. Each and every student, each and every class, mattered to me. I was convinced that we literally had to change the way teachers teach and the way schools were organized to help educationally disadvantaged kids learn in the optimal way for them. Moreover, we had to alter societal attitudes toward people with disabilities. Viewing myself as a potential agent for change, I devoted one entire lecture to emphasizing how adverse labeling affects people with disabilities. But was I getting my point across? Uncertainty gripped me.

"In my opinion," I told my class, "we cannot justify using general disability labels like 'cerebral palsy,' 'emotionally disturbed,' or 'mentally retarded' in the classroom or school building. What a teacher really needs to know is a child's individual learning needs and style! Just because a child has been pegged as 'learning disabled' doesn't mean he or she learns in the same way or has the same educational needs as the thousands of other students with learning disabilities in our nations' schools."

To illustrate my theme, I chose a dramatic example, posing a rhetorical question: "How would you feel if you had cancer, and your professors and classmates referred to you as the 'Cancer Victim?" I asked. Then I inquired, "Excuse me, Cancer Victim, would you please discuss your term paper with the class today?"

I continued: "We can all agree that good teaching requires some knowledge of a student's medical condition so that the instructor can make the necessary adjustments. For example, a student may need to stand or move around if he is uncomfortable. Or, she may need to miss classes because of chemotherapy treatments. But wouldn't it be devastating if a professor were to depersonalize you as a 'Cancer Victim' - broadcasting it to everyone in the class? Is there a person in this class who would not feel abashed and dehumanized if not spoken of or to by name?"

Interpreting the facial expressions of the students, I decided that my diatribe was provocative and had impact. One student challenged my ideas:

After all, when a pejorative label is replaced with a kinder label, the kinder label will eventually take on a negative connotation. Take the term 'mental subnormality.' It was replaced with the term 'mental retardation' in the late fifties, then 'mental retardation' became 'person with a cognitive delay,' which also radiated negativity, so what's next? What's in a name? Will changing epithets really change the underlying problem? Will it really change people's attitudes to simply reword or rearrange the label?

This student was asking reasonable questions. Perhaps, I thought, my impassioned arguments were inappropriate in the college classroom, which traditionally is supposed to be dispassionate. My intention had been to make a scholarly presentation. Had I strayed from the factual research into hyperbole? My objective was to enumerate the pros and cons of labeling and stereotyping and present a balanced overview of the latest research and expert opinions. I knew we had just scratched the surface of an exceedingly complex and touchy issue. Then I reflected on the degradation of the slaves in the Antebellum South, whose owners sought to remove their personhood and thus eliminate resistance by refusing to allow them surnames.

Continuing up the hill toward my office in my characteristically determined and rapid pace, I closed the gap between myself and the three people ahead of me. My reverie was interrupted by the stark image of a woman I was slowly overtaking. She had a familiar gait, reminiscent of the children I had worked with in the past. Perhaps it was the way in which her feet toed out or her flat-footed walk. Rapidly piecing together these visual cues with my academic and professional experience, I tried to track down the mental association.

Scottie, I thought, Yes! Her walk reminds me of Scottie!

Scottie was a delightful young student with Down syndrome in my special education class years ago in West Virginia. A chubby and sociable eleven year-old, she was the oldest of five daughters whose family lived in a coal-mining town. Her I.Q. tested in the moderate range of mental retardation, yet she was reading at the second grade level. Although she was quite verbal, sometimes she was difficult to understand because of her speech articulation problems.

I contemplated my linkage of Scottie with the woman in front of me. This older woman was about 5 feet tall, with legs that seemed relatively thin in comparison with her rather stout upper body. I wondered if her neck were thick and short like Scottie's. Because I was approaching her from behind, my association was only speculation. I looked more intently, but her belongings contradicted my hunch. She was carrying a notebook and textbooks just like any other university student would. My curiosity was getting the better of me, so I shifted my walk into high gear to pass her.

The young woman was wearing glasses, with sweatshirt, sweat pants, and stocking cap suggesting a tomboyish outlook. Curly auburn hair looped around the borders of her cap. Could she possibly be a student? Yes, it was possible - student attire was definitely more casual in the eighties than in previous decades. The standard uniform was jeans and a flannel shirt or sweatshirt - even for women.

I would have to test my intuition with a closer look, I thought. Since she was well ahead of me, I practically had to run to overtake her. Turning my head to get a good look as I passed, I could see the features that confirmed my suspicions...

Fortunately, the woman didn't seem to notice my furtive gaze. Perhaps, I hypothesized, she was so used to stares that they no longer seemed worthy of attention. I had always deplored it when others would gaze insensitively at another person when they sensed something was out of the ordinary. Now I was guilty of this unseemly behavior my-self. Should I say something? Should I introduce myself? Would it be patronizing to strike up a conversation with her just because she might have a disability? I decided to say nothing and continued the walk to my office.

The following week, I was having lunch in the university snack bar with another professor. We were having our usual discussion, com-plaining about malfunctioning overhead projectors or about our outrageously low salaries. After spending two years in a master's degree program and four years in a doctoral program, I was earning a whop-ping faculty salary of $18,000 a year. Would we ever climb out of debt incurred through loss of salary and student loans? Would we ever be able to do significant research with our course overloads?

Then I saw her again. She was sitting at a table, drinking coke and conversing with several university students. Jovial laughter pealed out from their table as they began to gather their backpacks and coats. A bell rang; she hurried off, probably to her next class.

This second encounter forced me to abandon my whining about trivia, finances and academic red tape. This time I was able to glean more visual clues. What was it about her face? Was her body out of proportion? Could it be the set of her eyes? Perhaps it was her facial structure. Certainly her voice had a unique quality. In addition to being several decibels above everyone else's at her table, it was strained and raspy. I guessed she was in her late twenties. Her skin was soft and freckled, her smile wide and vulnerable. Her exuberance stood out among the more reserved Maine students. There was an immature, youthful quality to her jocularity. I simply had to meet her.

I grabbed my briefcase and approached one of the students still seated at the table.

"I know this is awkward, but I couldn't help noticing the woman you were sitting with, and I wondered if you could introduce me to her sometime? I'm JoAnne Putnam, a faculty member in the special education department."

"Oh, you mean Paige Barton? Sure, she'll probably be here tomorrow. If you're here then, I'll introduce you."

The next day I found both students at the same table in the snack bar, and Paige and I were introduced. I asked her if she could stop by my office in Merrill Hall the next day. She said yes, and that she would leave a message with the secretary about the time she would be there.

Unbelievable, I thought, as I returned to my office. I was close to reaching for the phone to call Dr. Rynders, my doctoral advisor from the University of Minnesota and an internationally known expert on Down syndrome. We had collaborated on a chapter about characteristics and services for adults with Down syndrome in the book *Down syndrome: Creative Directions in Biomedicine and the Behavioral Sciences.* Here I was in my first college faculty position, and I had encountered a woman with Down syndrome attending my own university!

Dr. Rynder's research supported the finding that variation occurs in the intellectual abilities of people with Down syndrome. While most affected children whose intelligence is assessed fall within the mild to moderate range of retardation, researchers have identified children who test in the normal and above normal ranges. I imagined that he would be very excited to know about a woman with Down syndrome who was capable of college level work. But I restrained myself from calling until I could find out if she really did have the syndrome.

That afternoon Paige arrived at my office punctually. She was casually dressed, neat and clean. Her eyes, hazel and framed by large rimmed glasses, drew my first close look. There was an unusual shape to her pupil, which looked almost like an old fashioned keyhole. I wondered whether she had sustained an eye injury. She had freckles and short auburn hair, permed in tight coils, a style so popular with old ladies who frequent beauty parlors.

I detected a very slight articulation problem that might have been due to poor dentition. Her front teeth were yellowed and in need of new caps, but aesthetics didn't prevent her from smiling broadly.

Her eyes sparkled when she spoke of her college education. Her cheeks were dimpled, and she had a casual manner that conveyed a lack of self-consciousness. I discerned an innocent naivete in her unassuming, jocular manner - unsophisticated, yet pure. What a refreshing contrast to the measured cautious, self-promotion, and arrogance I had often encountered in university settings.

"Tell me about your major," I said, opening the conversation with a somewhat trite query.

"I'm majoring in early childhood education," she explained, "and I'm about half way through the associate's degree program, which takes two years."

"Why early childhood?" I probed.

"For as long as I can remember, I've wanted to work with young children either in a day care, a preschool, or Head Start. Most of all I want to work with young children with special needs," she explained.

"Have you had any experience with children with disabilities?" I asked.

"Well, when I was at Apple Creek, I got to work with young children in a crib ward, and I really enjoyed it."

"Apple Creek?" I questioned.

"Yes, when I was a teenager, I was a patient aide at the Apple Creek State Hospital. It's an institution."

The word institution staggered me. Sitting in my office was a woman, a student at the university, who appeared to have Down syndrome and had been institutionalized! I continued my questioning, trying to ascertain whether she really had the academic background to attend a university.

"From which high school did you get your degree?"

"Well," she paused, "I didn't actually get to go to high school, but I took my G.E.D. test in 1979 and passed it."

"The truth is," she continued, "my family is against my decision to attend UMF. They think it's too expensive. They're sure I'll never get out from under the student loans I'm taking out. But no one believed I could get my G.E.D., but I tried anyway. And I did it! I proved them wrong! And I'm going to do it again," she said with a rebellious conviction.

Oh no, I thought, here's a woman who was institutionalized, didn't go to high school, and only has a G.E.D. And now she wants a university degree? As if Down syndrome weren't enough of an onus, add to that no high school education. I doubted that she had the academic prerequisites to succeed. All the odds were stacked against her. I wondered why she didn't attend a trade school or a technical college.

"So," I asked bluntly, "How are your grades?"

"Fine," she said, "I have a B minus average."

Nothing wrong with that, I thought. Still, her case just didn't make sense. She was an anomaly, someone who had spent her high school years wasting away in an institution rather than being educated, and now she was striving for a university degree.

My mind wandered back to my introductory class in special education. The next week I planned to cover the historical aspects of special education services. I wondered if she would be a good speaker about institutions. What would it hurt to take a chance? I asked myself.

"I wonder if you'd be willing to make a presentation to my class about your experiences?" Paige's reply was unforgettable:

"No way," she said. "There is no way I can get up in front of a class and talk." NO WAY!" she repeated.

"But I think you'll be a good speaker," I rejoined. "And, from what I already know about you, I think you have an important message to share with future special educators. By telling your story, you could make a difference in how they teach and ultimately in the lives of children down the road."

I think bringing up children was what convinced her. She said, "Let me think about it. Can I call you tomorrow?"

The next day she called, reluctantly agreeing to meet with my class the following week.

Before class on Tuesday afternoon, I asked if I could videotape the talk. She said it would be OK, in case I wanted to use it in other classes. But the prospect of being taped heightened her anxiety. Just before class, a button popped off the waistband of her skirt, and we had to pin the skirt together. But she kept her sense of humor and we giggled about the mishap.

If she makes it through this hour without falling apart, it will be amazing, I thought. I wasn't sure that she could handle the pressure. But Paige took her place at the front of the classroom, sitting casually on the instructor's desk with a microphone strapped around her neck. Looking very respectable, if not preppy, she wore a black and white plaid wool skirt and a black silk blouse. Her white boots were lined with fur. "Hello, my name is Paige Barton, and I have mosaic Down syndrome" she began. You could have heard a pin drop after she started talking; the students were absolutely captivated.

I knew something magical was happening in the classroom. Paige had an outline for her talk, but she simply set it aside, looked directly at her audience and began speaking extemporaneously - from the heart.

With segregated facilities still fresh in her mind from six years before, she started describing her transition into the community. She shared her opinions about the misguided placement of children with Down syndrome in isolated facilities and alluded to tensions with her family regarding her ability to live in the community independently.

> *If I can do nothing else, I'd like to get out there and give some parents of Down syndrome children some hope. And just ... to try to stop what happened to me from happening to other kids with Down syndrome. There are those who would like right now to put me back into an institution again, so I'm thankful that*

they can't do this... again.

*And I think that I've proven to a whole lot of people
that you can't say that a Down syndrome person
would never be able to do anything. I had someone
say that to me in September of this year who was
a friend of mine (she no longer is because she was
knocking down what I was doing) . . . she said to
me that a Down syndrome will never graduate from
college. I said I didn't need to hear that right now
because I was going to be graduating in May. I said
I think I've proven to a whole lot of people that we
can do things if we put our minds to it.*

Paige told about "accepting the Lord" about two weeks after she was
released from the institution and how it turned her life around. "If
we put our minds...to doing something and if we have the help of the
Lord, we can do it. I may have lost a family because all of my brothers
and sisters are on my mother's side too, but I've gained one I can't lose
- and that's the church."

She talked about a child with Down syndrome in the early intervention
program she was particularly fond of. She admired this child's mother
who had been told by the pediatrician to send him away to an institution when he was born. The mother refused, and was raising him as a
single parent.

I was spellbound with her story, which was far more dramatic than I
could have imagined. To end her speech, Paige told the students that
she had been taking a course in sign language and would like to sign a

song. She turned on her tape recorder that rested on the desk beside her. A hush came over the room.

Paige signed the words to the gospel song "Touch Through Me" by Dottie Rambo. Paige loved this moving song and its message that the Holy Spirit works though people when they reach out to help and care for others.

I felt a swelling in my throat and tears were welling up in my eyes. The speech and the song evoked a profound emotional response that I had not expected - a response I was to experience whenever I heard Paige speak. Half-embarrassed, I blinked back my tears as I scanned the rows of my students. Some were searching into their backpacks and purses to find tissues to wipe away their tears. Even the more controlled male students were visibly moved. She had touched us all very deeply.

Paige seemed transformed when she spoke. She organized her thoughts so naturally, yet so effectively in communicating her message. She spoke with an ease that I had never possessed as a public speaker or lecturer. More important, her story and her message were both heart-rending and compelling. I was imagining her speaking at special education conferences, speaking to parents, speaking to community members. . .

After class she asked me if she did okay. "OK?" I replied. "You were better than OK, you were great! Your story is amazing, and you spoke so naturally. I wonder if you would give this talk again?

"Let's get together next week," I suggested. "Do you have time for coffee? I'd love to hear about your childhood."

Chapter 4

Little Dynamo

> *One young man with Down syndrome was asked to*
> *define retarded. He said he meets with people who*
> *see he is different and who can't communicate with*
> *him and are unable to get their "love flow" going.*
> *"They're retarded," he said.*
> -Bernie S. Siegel, Prescriptions for Living

Paige was born to Betty Jane and Gene Barton on October 25, 1951. She weighed 6 pounds, 6 ounces and was delivered by an outstanding obstetrician in the Magee-Women's Hospital of Pittsburgh, Pennsylvania. The birth was typical and the pregnancy uncomplicated.

At three months of age and again at six months, Paige came down with bronchial pneumonia. Unbeknownst to the family, the physicians suspected that she was, in the terminology of the day, a "mongol." Written across an early medical chart were the words, "Watch this one carefully - suspected Mongoloid."

"I didn't know exactly what the word meant," said Paige's mother when interviewed on the Today Show, "but it had a bad feel to it. You know, like she wasn't going to live very long." "Anyway, what did it matter what she had? She just needed more medical care, more of this, more of that."

As a result of Paige's early illnesses, she was small and developed slowly. Thankfully, the Barton children either weren't aware or weren't terribly concerned with their little sister's unusual features or tiny size. Perhaps children from large families tend to be more accepting of diversity and differences and are less inclined to put undue focus on one sibling's particular problems or uniqueness. At the time of her birth, Paige's sisters' ages ranged from 14 months to 10 years, with a 4, 7, and 8 year old in between. She was the sixth daughter. Four more siblings, three of them boys, would join the Barton family in the years ahead.

The Bartons' home on Shady Avenue in Pittsburgh was huge, with ten bedrooms and four floors, if one counts the basement. This glorious, red brick house situated on a tree-lined street was perfect for a family of twelve. Paige was more than satisfied with her bedroom on the third floor with the older girls, especially because not all of her siblings had their own rooms. The Barton's basement was a community drawing card for endless games of ping-pong. The neighborhood was bustling with children - certainly no shortage of playmates - and was as near as one can get to a child's paradise, according to Paige.

Little Paige was a toddler of about 2 1/2 when her developmental status was assessed at a facility operated by the Catholic Church. According to the report, Paige's intelligence quotient, or I.Q., was 55. An average I.Q. score was 100, so 55 was considered "subnormal," and in the "trainable mentally retarded" range. It was understood that the results of the I.Q. tests had to be interpreted with caution because Paige was really too young to be assessed with any accuracy. But the use of the terms subnormal and mentally retarded conveyed a deep pessimism about the toddler's future. In the 1950's, one's I.Q. was considered to be a stable attribute, so a "subnormal" I.Q. offered little prospect for improvement through maturation or by remediation.

The evaluators recommended that Paige attend a nursery school the following year, and she was enrolled in the Presbyterian Church School, where she spent two years. Then she entered the Linden School in the Pittsburgh Public School District for two years of kindergarten and then for two years in first grade, suffering the minor stigma of repeating first grade.

Paige's hazy memories of Linden Elementary School were positive. In step with her older sisters, she was enrolled in Miss Pollard's first grade class. Miss Pollard was an ideal teacher, always patient and kind. She was a dedicated professional who took a personal interest in all her students - and Paige was no exception. Miss Pollard was ingenious in devising clever ways of assisting Paige's learning and development. She found "fat" chalk for writing on the blackboard, wide pencils that provided a good grip for printing and drawing, and wide-lined paper that better accommodated Paige's unsteady and uncoordinated movements as she laboriously formed letters. Paige's hands were small, and her fingers were chubby, making manipulative tasks more of an obstacle for her than for the other first graders.

At the end of the school year, Miss Pollard recommended that Paige be retained in first grade so that she would have additional time to acquire a firm foundation for academics. With an additional year in first grade, Miss Pollard felt that Paige would fully master the prerequisite skills necessary for second grade.

Paige's reaction was positive. She actually relished the thought of spending another year with her beloved, creative teacher. She was determined to learn to read, print, and do math with as much facility as the other first graders.

But by third grade it was becoming more difficult for her to keep up with the rest of her classmates. Socially, she was having trouble fitting in. By about third or fourth grade children become more conventional in their thinking and begin to make judgments about one another, often rigidly insisting on strict behavior norms. They begin to draw boundaries around their chosen circle of friends to the exclusion of others. In this case, it was Paige who was excluded. As Paige matured, she gained greater awareness of herself and others. With her increasing depth of emotion, she became more vulnerable to the sting of rejection.

Paige's intimations of her inadequacy were further confirmed when her brother Peter was placed in her third grade room. In actuality, Peter was technically Paige's cousin, but because they were raised together, she thought of him as a brother. Peter was eight and Paige was nine, an indignity to the sensitive Paige. In her words:

> *I couldn't figure out why he ended up in my class when he was younger than I was. And to make matters worse, he was put in a higher reading group. At first I thought I just wasn't trying hard enough at my schoolwork. Then it sank in, and, for the first time, I wondered if there was something wrong with my brain.*

Kids could be quite cruel in the early sixties, as they still are, especially if they detect a human weakness or a difference that they don't understand. Paige's classmates were becoming less tolerant of her shortcomings and her uniqueness. Although having Peter in her class underscored the fact that she wasn't keeping up, upon reflection, she recognized that there were some advantages to his presence.

> *When the kids teased me, Peter was my champion.*
> *He was also the class clown, which created problems*
> *for the teacher, but made school more bearable for*
> *me. When I was upset or when my feelings were hurt,*
> *Peter could always make me smile and laugh.*

Ultimately, Paige decided that the benefits of having Peter as her advocate and protector outweighed the disappointment of knowing that he had progressed beyond her intellectually. A strong bond was forming with Peter, which would carry Paige through more troubled times yet to come.

In 1962, Paige's father was transferred from his job at the U.S. Steel Homestead Plant in Pittsburgh to the Jones and Laughlin Steel plant in Cleveland, Ohio. The family would have to relocate to North Madison, a nearby town. Paige remembered how difficult it was for her to leave their home on Shady Avenue, but no questions were asked. Because Paige's father was the financial supporter of the family, his work had to come first.

Just before the Bartons left Pittsburgh and Linden Elementary School, a psychologist from the Pittsburgh School District evaluated Paige. An individual I.Q. test was administered, yielding an overall I.Q. of 89. Eighty-nine was slightly below average, but still within the normal range and a whopping 34 points higher than the estimate of a 55 obtained when she was 2 1/2. Consequently, the school administrators from Pittsburgh recommended that she attend regular fourth grade in Ohio. It took some courage, but her mother decided to simply enroll Paige, like any other newcomer, in the North Madison Redbird Middle School.

In the early sixties most educators were too intimidated by the I.Q. test's aura of infallibility to doubt its accuracy. They brushed aside the problems I.Q. tests presented to test takers with learning differences and discarded the value of environment and education in raising an individual's score. Like having poor eyesight or a missing finger, a low I.Q. was thought to haunt and impede a person throughout life because it was an unchanging heritable trait.

Moving to a new town and establishing new friendships can be wrenching for anyone, but for Paige the move was doubly challenging. She not only had to adjust to a new school but also had to endure the stares and curiosity about her unusual appearance. Nonetheless, she successfully completed fourth and fifth grade. However, several months into sixth grade, her adjustment problems were becoming more pronounced. She needed increasing degrees of instructional support to bolster her academic skills in order to keep pace with her classmates.

In the course of searching for possible solutions to Paige's learning problems, the Bartons heard about a special education class for children with academic handicaps. It seemed like the only option at the time.

In the fall of 1965 Paige was removed from her sixth grade class and enrolled in a special education program in the Painesville Township of Lake County, about 45 minutes from the Bartons' home. With so many children and obligations, driving for an hour and a half each day represented a significant time commitment for Paige's mother. Yet she never really gave the driving time or the expense a second thought, simply doing what needed to be done on behalf of her child. Unfortunately, the time investment and the added expense of transporting Paige to this "special" class turned out to be a waste of time and resources. The program was a major disappointment. Rather than receiving the extra tutoring and intensive, personalized instruction she needed to succeed in the regular classroom, Paige spent her time rehashing work that she had already mastered. Her school days were misspent in boredom and repetition, and she was falling even further behind her classmates.

Paige detested the Painesville special education class. There was such a stark contrast between the environment of her orderly regular classrooms and that of the special education room.

The special education class was disheveled - messy, disorganized, filthy, and unfit for children. It showed how schools devalued children with learning problems. "I guess this was my first encounter with discrimination against kids with learning disabilities," recalled Paige ruefully.

Curiously, only a few decades ago, no one seemed to question the irony of society's practice of relegating those students already challenged by learning problems to inferior instruction in the poorest of environmental circumstances. However, what Paige couldn't have known then is that, of the hundreds of thousands of children with disabilities, she was one of the lucky ones who was privileged to attend school. In the 1960's most children with disabilities were flatly denied the opportunity of an education; they stayed sequestered at home or were shunted aside, dispatched to institutions. At that time Paige couldn't have fathomed the alternative of being placed in an institution away from her loved ones.

Even though the academic year was not quite over, Ms. Barton saw no point in continuing Paige in the inferior special program. She astutely returned her to Redbird Elementary in May. It was promised that Redbird would be establishing a new special education class the following year. Unfortunately, it turned out that the class was designed for children younger than Paige. Again, Paige's I.Q. was tested again. This time the score was 84, a slight drop from her prior 89.

Summers spent on the beach swimming and playing with her brothers and sisters at Lake Erie were Paige's happiest and most carefree times. During the winters, the children would go sledding for hours on a hill by the beach. Paige remembered one frigid December day climbing to the top of the hill in her rubber boots. She hopped on her Red Flyer sled, giving it that extra push for a fast take off. The conditions that day were exceptionally conducive to sledding, hard packed snow with a glaze of ice. During this particular run the sled propelled Paige farther than she expected, and she flashed past the shore of the icy lake where the sled usually stopped. Before she knew it, she was careening over the ice when she heard a loud cracking beneath her. Unable to change the course of the runaway sled, she was immersed in freezing water.

Brother Peter was near, but he had his own priorities, the first being to rescue the Red Flyer. Fortunately for Paige, the water was shallow enough that she could help herself out onto the shore. Freezing, she managed to run home, soaked and shaking with chills.

Like most children, Paige was exposed to the risks that were simply a part of growing up. She was a genuine member of a large and loving family of 12, experiencing the same rough and tumble childhood as the other siblings. She wasn't treated preferentially, so her childhood was filled with the typical bumps and bruises, broken arms, and cuts most children suffered in those days.

One of her injuries she remembered well was a black eye from a dangerously misguided baseball bat. The responsible party, a neighborhood bully, claimed it was an accident, but Paige was convinced that the wild pitch was intentional.

> *I was at a picnic with my sister Wendy. We were playing ball with some other kids when I walked behind the batter to get a drink of water. The pitcher saw me there, but he threw the ball anyway. The batter knew I was there, but he swung the bat and hit me in the eye. I had two black eyes from this. They thought I might go blind, but I was taken to an opthamologist and treated. Eventually, the sight in my left eye started deteriorating to the point where I have almost no vision in that eye.*

At age nine, Paige was badly cut by glass in a skirmish with her brother. As Paige recalled, Peter had locked her out of the house, so she tried to get in by putting her arm through a window pane in the door. According to the operation record at the hospital, she had a severe laceration of the wrist and her median nerve was "3/4 divided" through its entire circumference. Fortunately, the doctors were able to repair the nerve. Interestingly, and unbeknownst to her, it was noted in that medical report that Paige was "mongolian."

Paige remembered a birthday party she had the first year they were
in North Madison. She was too new to the area to have made many
friends, but birthday invitations were sent to all of her classmates. The
house was decorated and a birthday cake prepared. Dressed in her
party clothes, Paige eagerly waited for the children to arrive. Sadly, the
only one who came to her birthday party that afternoon was Annie,
a neighborhood girl. No one else showed up. Decades later, in 1996
after the Today Show aired a segment on Paige, Annie called her from
California. She told Paige that she had a son with cerebral palsy and
that she was inspired by Paige's story.

Despite the many challenges Paige faced as a young girl - respiratory
infections, poor physical coordination, learning problems, and social
rejection because of her unusual appearance, she felt she had a happy
childhood.

Fundamental to Paige's development was the Barton family's religious
life. Every Sunday the family went to church. Even when the parents
were unable to attend, the children would go together. In Pennsylvania
they attended a Presbyterian church, and in Ohio a Congregational
church. Paige fondly reminisced about the part she played in the annual Christmas pageants. Most often she enacted an angel holding a
battery operated candle. As a young child, Paige established a spiritual
foundation that carried her through some very difficult years to come.
Little did she know that one day she would appear as an angel to others
- but without the battery operated candle.

As time progressed, Paige's schoolwork and life in the community
became more difficult. Although the sixth grade teacher at Redbird
Middle School felt Paige had not fully mastered the work that year, she

recommended moving her into the 7th grade anyway.

Hindsight is always 20/20. Many current educators postulate that the 7th grade curriculum represents a far greater leap ahead in the degree of difficulty of verbal and math concepts introduced than those in earlier grades. For Paige to have been pushed ahead without full comprehension of 6th grade work translated into treacherous academic shoals ahead for the girl, especially with her already-present learning differences.

One afternoon after school, Paige came into the house crying.

"What in the world happened? " asked her mother.

Paige was sobbing as she replied. "The kids keep teasing me. They call me Monkey. Mom, do I look like a monkey?"

"Of course not!" Ms. Barton retorted emphatically.

In spite of her mother's reassurance, it was apparent that Paige was having difficulty adjusting to the more complicated routine of Redbird Middle School. Changing classes each period was especially confusing. She was intimidated by the science teacher and stretched beyond her limit in physical education. Snickering classmates didn't help matters, and even though she was small, she felt awkward being 14 years old and only in the seventh grade.

"I remember trying to walk on the balance beam. I kept falling off. But I would get back on and try again - over and over and over - until I could do it." Determination and an unwillingness to give up were qualities that Paige exhibited early on, and which persisted throughout her life.

Paige was even known to be stubborn as a baby in the playpen. She would stiffen and throw herself down on the mat in protest when she didn't get her way. Though we now glibly speak of the prevalence of rage in the decade of the 2000's, Paige was probably demonstrating perseverance, not temper.

According to family members, Paige was never a pushover, even as a young child. Once when she and brother Peter were told to go to bed, he refused by saying, "No, I won't." Paige's reply to him was a vociferous "The hell you're not!"

But for all of Paige's determination, it became more difficult for her to succeed academically in middle school. Moreover, the social isolation and snubs Paige experienced in the neighborhood were very troubling to her parents. It was an era of segregation, and very little tolerance of diversity. Unfortunately, many children had little experience with students with disabilities, which resulted in stereotyping and unfortunate prejudices. Something had to be done, so a meeting was scheduled with the school principal, and an appointment was made with the family doctor to discuss Paige's predicament.

Both the principal and the physician gave the same feeble advice: place Paige in a school that specialized in children with disabilities. They said Paige was slow and that she would never be able to keep up with her classmates' progress. It didn't seem right to continue to subject Paige to defeats at school plus ridicule from her peers, they added.

Despite everyone's grave concerns about Paige's academic performance, Paige claimed that her grades actually were average - mostly B's, C's, and a few D's. These grades were acceptable at a time before "grade inflation," when a C actually meant "average."

Weighing the opinions of educators, physicians, and relatives, it was decided that Paige should be placed in a special school. Conceding her inability to mainstream her daughter, in January of '67, Ms. Barton wrote to a social worker who was assisting them in their quest to find the right situation for Paige.

The letter reported Paige's I.Q. scores and described her educational history, noting that she had failed to advance in the special class. Her physical handicaps were listed, including a "keyhole retina" in one eye with little or no sight, thumb sucking, bed wetting, and dental problems. It explained away Paige's test performance, which was not poor enough to warrant institutionalization. "Paige tested higher than she really is...with a large group at home...tests are no problem to her."

The overriding concern was that she "be trained to do some routine task" and have a home base should something happen to them. Training, they felt, was more important than schooling at this point. The letter stated that Paige was a "dear little girl" and expressed the concern that she might live a lonesome life.

Advice was also sought from a physician who enjoyed an excellent reputation as a medical expert. His recommendation was to contact the Home for Crippled Children in Pittsburgh about enrolling Paige. It wasn't certain that Paige would be accepted, however, because she really wasn't physically "crippled."

The Home for Crippled Children had an excellent reputation as a rehabilitation facility specializing in the education of children with physical disabilities. It was considered to be a fine facility, funded by the Mellon Foundation. In addition to evaluating Paige, they were going to fix her teeth. Before entering the home, Paige had a large gap between her front teeth which the dentists at the Home corrected. The only drawback was the Home's long distance from the Bartons' home. The Bartons decided that Paige would and should attend school at the Home for Crippled Children - immediately.

"Immediately" was an icy day in February, 1967, and Paige had just boarded the school bus for home. Paige described the scene many times over the years in her speeches. As the bus was about to depart, Peter appeared, telling his sister "Get off the bus! Mom wants you!" Sure enough, there was her mother, standing in front of the school.

"Go in and clean out your locker," she was told. Obediently, Paige went into the school and emptied her locker, perplexed about why she was leaving. Optimistically, she speculated that she would now be attending an all-girls private school, like her older sisters. With her school belongings removed from the locker, she went home. Three days later, she was on her way to Pittsburgh.

Paige claimed that her father was uncomfortable with the decision to place her in the Home for Crippled Children. Yet chance decreed that he was out of commission when his daughter was sent away. Paige reported,

> *I can remember my father trying to talk my mom out*
> *of it, but he was involved in an automobile accident*

the night they took me to Pittsburgh. It was a serious
accident and all of his teeth were knocked out. But
I didn't find out about the accident until about six
weeks later. It shows how my family tried to shield
me from things that might upset me.

Overprotection and shielding were themes that continued to disturb Paige throughout her life, especially in her relationship with her father, to whom she felt very close. Paige continued:

I had visitors while at the Children's Home, and my
sister Wendy who lived in Pittsburgh came once a
week and also took me home with her whenever she
could. They put me in a class at the home and I did
really well. But I was only at Crippled Children's for
about six months when I was taken back home. I
thought I was going back to the regular school and to
live at home.

Paige was wrong.

Chapter 5

Birds in Cages

> *God didn't mean for us to be in a cage, but to fly and*
> *reach the highest heights we can.*
>
> -Paige Barton

Paige's stay at the pleasant Home for Crippled Children was all-too-short-lived, lasting only six months. She certainly did not fit the profile of the typical resident of Crippled Children's, almost all of whom had some kind of physical disability, such as cerebral palsy or an orthopedic impairment. As it turned out, the actual purpose of placing Paige there was to conduct an evaluation of her "mental capacities" which would determine whether she would be a good candidate for placement at the state institution. The Home's pediatrician responsible for the Crippled Children's admitting report, dated January 13, 1967, wrote the following pessimistic appraisal. Plainly, his judgment was clouded by earlier evaluations of Paige's capacities.

> *Indeed, there has been some question as to whether*
> *this girl was eligible for state school or whether she*
> *could do some job outside of state school. She may*
> *have some physical disabilities that may furthermore*
> *still put her at a disadvantage, so a complete work up*
> *must be done.*

The pediatrician concluded that Paige had "stigmata of mongolism" and that she should have audiologic testing, chromosomal studies, visual perceptual testing, and psychological testing.

Far from its religious meaning, stigmata is the plural of the word stigma, which refers to "a mark indicative of a history of disease or abnormality," according to *Webster's II College Dictionary*. During the 1950s and '60s, many believed that the "stigmata" of Paige's disorder, such as slanted eyes and straight hair, resembled the features of the Mongolian race - thus it was referred to as mongolism. In 1866, London physician Langdon Down first identified the cluster of symptoms characteristic of the disorder now referred to as Down syndrome, or Trisomy 21. While his observations of the disorder are classic, he erroneously explained its origin as a reversion to a primitive racial type. Even more disturbing was Crookshank's declaration in his book *A Mongol in our Midst* (1924) that the syndrome was a reversion to the orangutan. Finally, in 1959, after decades of research on cell biology and chromosomal analysis, Lejeune and his colleagues identified 47 chromosomes rather than the usual 46 in the tissue cultures of "mongoloid" children. It took almost two more decades before the National Down Syndrome Congress advocated for the use of "Down syndrome" and advised dropping the term mongolism altogether.

In the sixties, a clinical diagnosis of mongolism was sufficient to justify institutional placement. It was almost universally assumed that all persons with Down syndrome were moderately to severely retarded. We now know, of course, that this assumption was erroneous. In 1978, John Rynders, my doctoral advisor, reviewed 15 studies which showed a significant range of functioning on the intelligence test scores of children with Down syndrome, including scores within the normal range. But in 1967, it was not surprising that the evaluation team at the Home for Crippled Children found that Paige should forever dwell in a twilight zone, the state institution.

After the Bartons had sifted through the reports and agonized over making the right decision, they ultimately decided that state school was in everyone's best interest. In an era when genetic testing was in its infancy, parents rarely second-guessed the pronouncements of medical experts.

In August of 1967, Ms. Barton reluctantly filled out the paper work required for admission to Apple Creek State Hospital in Apple Creek, Ohio. Among the many forms she completed, one requested an abbreviated case history. In responding to an item soliciting "pertinent facts in family history," written wistfully, almost in terms of emotional surrender, it told how Paige was one of ten children who had been kept home because of their love for her and their wish for her to benefit from family relationships. But the younger children were now surpassing her in accomplishments and they believed she would be happier with children of "a more equal nature" and where she could be trained to do things at her own level.

Ms. Barton clearly had qualms about giving up her child and misgivings about the institutional placement. She hoped that they had made the proper decision, writing that the family's loss would be the institution's gain, "as Paige has always been a joy to be near."

In 1967, according to the "Indeterminate Order of Hospitalization" document, Paige was to be placed in Apple Creek State Hospital, a state supported residential hospital for people with mental retardation and mental illness. In 1931, the school was founded as the "Apple Creek School for the Feeble Minded," intended for those with mental retardation. In 1949 its mission was expanded to serve individuals with mental illness as well. Then, in 1972, it reverted back to a mental retardation facility.

Because Paige's physicians and family were concerned about her intellectual problems and the "stigmata of mongolism," it would hardly seem appropriate to have cooped Paige up in an institution that also served people who were mentally ill. However, Apple Creek was the only facility in the vicinity available at the time for those adjudged "different." All too quickly, society relegated people to institutional "holding areas" if they functioned idiosyncratically - or in Paige's case - did not appear "normal," regardless of the causes.

Earlier in the 1960s, President John F. Kennedy, whose sister Rosemary was diagnosed as having mental retardation, championed change in the care and treatment of people with mental illness or mental retardation, as well as those who were culturally deprived. During this period, media exposés of mental institutions divulged the depraved conditions and deplorable treatment of the residents. With photographer Fred Kaplan, Burton Blatt, a professor of education, author, and reformer, published the shocking photographic essay *Christmas in Purgatory*. They documented in text and photographs the horrifying conditions of the "backwards" in institutions for the mentally retarded. "Backwards" were areas of institutions forbidden to the public, so the exposé involved surreptitious photography by means of a camera hidden on Fred Kaplan's belt. Kaplan accompanied Blatt on visits to the "darkest corridors and vestibules that humanity provides for its journey to purgatory" (Blatt, 1981, p.141).

In 1965, Senator Robert Kennedy toured the shocking conditions of institutions in New York State, and the abysmal horror he encountered - along with his genuine tears - hit the media like a blitzkrieg. The public was stunned to learn that human beings were treated less humanely than animals in a shelter. Outrage manifested itself in ever-louder protests against the brutish treatment of people with mental retardation. Something, the public decreed, had to be done.

As policy makers pondered solutions, researchers and educators were beginning to believe that a link existed between poverty and mental illness/mental retardation. They were increasingly aware that the lack of proper stimulation and opportunity to learn plaguing impoverished rural and urban areas sometimes impeded a child's usual intellectual and emotional development. Both mental illness and mental retardation were then considered to be twin problems that might be curable through improvements in education - preschool through secondary.

When they were first established, institutions, or asylums, as they were called, were designed to protect people from the scorn and brutality of society. The purpose of the first asylums, such as Bicetre in Paris, founded in 1632 by Vincent de Paul - intended as sanctuaries for mentally ill, mentally retarded, blind, epileptic, and other disabled people - had been obscured by the ashes of three centuries (Evans, 1983). As asylums mushroomed in population, admitting criminals, the indigent, and other "deviants," they evolved into prisons of isolation and perennial confinement - the antithesis of sanctuary, the ash heap of life. Asylums became the embodiment of Dante's purgatory, over whose gates were inscribed the perfect words to epitomize hopelessness:

All hope abandon, ye who enter here.

Ms. Barton drove Paige to Apple Creek State Hospital on October 10th, 1967, a few weeks before her 16th birthday. Leaving all that was familiar, they departed the animated, bustling cities and crowded highways for the quiet country roads, about 70 miles southwest of Akron. Nearing the institution, Paige grew frightened of being banished to this remote setting. As she examined the foreboding brick buildings and the wooded grounds, she began to comprehend how removed she would be from her family, her friends, her home, her community - all that she was familiar with and loved. Rightly, she was afraid that it would be all too easy for everyone to forget her, stuck away in a mental no-man's-land.

Situated in north central Ohio, Apple Creek housed 2,500 patients on grounds that covered about 2,000 acres in the rolling, bucolic hills of Wayne County. Many institutions in rural areas were established as farm colonies where residents helped till the land that in turn supported the inhabitants. Paige knew by the length of the drive how remote this asylum/fortress was from any sizeable town. She would also become painfully aware of the many ways that this enclave was detached from the everyday world of the normal.

The massive brick dormitory buildings were bastions that kept the residents within their confines by locks on the doors to the entrances and the individual hallways. The locks on the outside of the doors to the rooms, opened only by institutional personnel, secured the people inside. Bars on the windows gave the dismal place the appearance of an impenetrable fortress, from which any escape was unlikely.

Who was being protected? The inmates or society? And from what possible harm? Most likely, the purpose of confinement in institutions was to relieve society of the perceived burden of caring for and educating people with mental illness and disabilities. It would be euphemistic and self-deceptive to consider institutions to have educational or therapeutic purposes; in the sixties and seventies they were custodial warehouses.

Ms. Barton parked the car and mother and daughter entered the intake building. Confused and bewildered, Paige was ushered into the special admissions ward. On arrival, all patients were photographed and assigned a number, as if they were inmates in a penitentiary. Holding a black chalkboard placard with Apple Creek State Hospital across the top, white chalk identified her as Barton Paige, age 16 (she was actually 15 at the time), patient number 402196. Ironically, the picture, which we later jokingly referred to as her "mug shot," displays a beaming smile. How little she really understood about the significance of her confinement in Apple Creek.

Paige spent her first month at Apple Creek on the barren admissions ward. There, residents were put through various intake and evaluation procedures. The ward consisted of a large room crammed with about a hundred cots, wall-to-wall. There was barely enough space for walking between the beds, much less for chairs, bedstands, lamps, or other furniture we normally associate with residential living. The cramped room served as both daytime and nighttime quarters for the new admits. Residents were not allowed to leave the building for meals. Food was brought in from a kitchen in another building and served in an adjacent room.

Hour after hour, day after day, Paige sat aimlessly on her hard cot whenever she was not being poked, prodded, or questioned as part of the evaluation procedure. The reasons for the intake evaluations were to determine the extent of a patient's mental retardation, his or her physical condition, and his or her "likes and dislikes."

The days at Apple Creek were regimented according to a military-like cadence. Actually, the military may have afforded more freedom than did this state institution, which was, in many obvious ways, operated like a prison. The institution's 5:30 am wake-up time seemed absurdly early to Paige. No opportunity existed for pursuing personal interests or hobbies, and no one was allowed off the grounds. In fact, Paige's world was restricted to her own building, with no way for her to open her mind to the life around her or even to the imaginative world of books.

With thousands of residents, overcrowding mandated no privacy. The institution was run as much like a factory as a jail. As in horror and POW films, attendants used hoses to wash down the residents, stripping any sense of dignity they might have clung to. The degradation Paige felt, especially in the admissions wing, was a harbinger of what was to be her plunge into the bizarre and hellish life of the institution.

Despite her excruciating initiation into Apple Creek, Paige's ward admission record states that she was "pleasant and cooperative during admission." In retrospect, the documents unwittingly forecast that Paige's innate nature was conducive to adaptability and a desire to learn. All she would need, wrote the head nurse, was "some help with self care."

How could the need for help with self-care have justified relegating her to an institution for the mentally retarded? The hypocrisy of our public policies and the philosophy of institutionalization were clearly evident in Paige's case. If all she needed was some help with self-care, why confine her in a facility that provided no training and education? When admitted into Apple Creek, Paige's formal education came to a halt. At best, Apple Creek State Hospital was an overcrowded custodial facility.

Paige remembers her very first meal in the institution. "They actually tried to feed me! They had been told that I couldn't feed or dress myself. But it didn't take them long to find out what I could and couldn't do for myself."

A physical examination during the intake addressed Paige's Down syndrome - however, the findings did not corroborate earlier diagnoses. An extract from the physician's report is intriguing in light of past speculations about Paige's condition.

> *The hands and fingers are abnormal and associated*
> *with this the nails and nail beds likewise are abnor-*
> *mal. The characteristics of the hands are similar to*
> *those of mongolism, however the general hand abnor-*
> *mality does not reveal a complete transverse palmar*
> *crease and is slightly atypical for the Mongoloid hand*
> *particularly in its finger formation. The skull is of*
> *normal symmetry, is oblong, and measures 21 inches*
> *in circumference.*

In describing Paige in the report's section on the "mouth," the physician wrote:

> *Patient has a high palate and some narrowing of the*
> *space between the lateral dental ridges, but the tongue*

is perfectly normal and in no way resembles a Mon-
goloid tongue - nor is the patient a mouth breather.

The doctor's report ended with the diagnosis of "multiple congenital anomalies associated with Von Recklinghausen's syndrome."

Von Recklinghausen's syndrome, also known as neurofibromatosis, is a genetic disorder involving the 17th chromosome and is characterized by spots and tumors on the skin along with nervous system, endocrine organs, and blood vessels involvement. That was the first and last time this particular diagnosis was ever attached to Paige. Most likely, the café-au-lait spots on her skin, which are a marker of the syndrome, led to the erroneous clinical diagnosis of neurofibromatosis.

While at Apple Creek, Paige was also diagnosed with mild retardation and labeled "dull normal" by a psychologist. At the time, the I.Q. (intelligence quotient) level used as a cut-off for mental retardation was 85. In 1969, Paige's I.Q. tested out on the Weschler Adult Intelligence Scale as a Verbal I.Q. of 101 (in the average range) and a performance I.Q. of 70 (in the subaverage range), with the Full Scale I.Q. of 87. 2.[1]

Currently, the commonly accepted definition of mental retardation

1: The Weschler scale conceives of intelligence as being composed of two scales, verbal and performance, yielding three composite scores: Verbal, Performance, and Full Scale. Both the verbal and performance scales are subdivided into smaller subtests, such as arithmetic, reading and similarities in the Verbal Scale and picture completion, block design and object assembly in the Performance Scale. The performance scale was designed to assess problem solving items that involve judgement, reasoning, and planning - all imbued with a motoric requirement. The WAIS was used most frequently as a clinical tool for diagnostic and treatment purposes.

uses an I.Q. of approximately 70 at the upper end as a cut-off score and a complex analysis of the individual's functioning and need for support in several life areas. Therefore, according to today's standards, Paige would never have been classified as "mildly retarded." Moreover, given her high level of adaptive skills such as personal independence, mobility, and personal responsibility, it is unlikely that she would have been so classified even if her I.Q. had been lower.

The psychologist's report noted, "The subtest score pattern on the WAIS indicates that this girl is not truly retarded, but subnormal in most areas, especially perceptual organization (block design and object assembly)..." The rank injustice of consigning Paige to a life-in-death never occurred to these so-called experts, for nothing is more blinding than lack of knowledge. Why Paige's visual problems (bi-lateral alternating strabismus which prevents fixating with either eye, and the injured left eye) were not taken into account by the psychologists conducting the assessments is a conundrum, as these visual problems would likely affect her performance in perceptual organization. Moreover, her earliest evaluations stressed the need for audiological assessments, because of her hearing impairments. For many years, her poor hearing had been neglected. In fact, she didn't receive hearing aids until she was in her thirties. The psychologist noted that her subnormal scores on the WAIS were offset by very high scores in Arithmetic and Digit Span. At age 16, her grade level in arithmetic was 9.3. She could add, subtract, multiply and divide fractions. Again, taking these disparities into account seemed to be far from the minds of Paige's evaluators.

Interestingly, the only therapies recommended on the initial admission report conducted by physicians and psychologists at Apple Creek were for "eye glasses" and "education." However, neither urgent need was fulfilled at Apple Creek.

Another item on the admission report form referred to "the patient's general condition." The blank spaces on Paige's report were filled with the words "nutrition good" and "no vermin." Head and body lice were an ever-present threat in the large warehouse institutions, as they would quickly be transmitted among the thousands of residents who were packed into such tight quarters. It appears that Paige's lice-free head and body were among her most noteworthy assets noted by the admissions evaluator.

On November 1st, almost a month after Paige entered the Admission Ward, the attending physician recommended in his treatment plan that she be moved to Ward 11 after Thanksgiving. She also was appointed to the position of Patient Aide. The Patient Aides were assigned to work with the young children with severe disabilities. The children's ward was perhaps the most depressing in the institution, with cribs arranged side-by-side and head-to-head. Young children without the ability to sit up or ambulate lay for hours at a time by themselves, with nothing to do, with no contact from others. They would moan and cry, calling out for attention if they could. Sometimes they would rock and sway, flap their hands, or bang their heads against the wooden cribs to create their own stimulation.

Wearing crisp blue and white uniforms, the Patient Aids assisted with the feeding, diapering, positioning, and general care of over ninety children. The pay was a measly $5.00 a month, but was a welcome sum that could be used to buy items from the institution's store, such as cakes of soap. The pay, however, had little to do with the rewards of being a Patient Aide. Working with these needful children infused meaning into Paige's life in the institution; she became very attached to them. Caregiving gave her an opportunity to contribute to the lives of others, and her altruistic tasks kept her sane in this insane world. Discovering a meaningful purpose at Apple Creek was fortunate, because Paige's sense of self-worth was precariously low and her spirit was to be nearly broken.

A Medical Madhouse

According to the institution's medical records, on November 24th, 1967, around the week of Thanksgiving, Paige was put on a regimen of Thorazine: 100 milligrams. Thorazine is a powerful antipsychotic drug that has been prescribed for the management of psychotic disorders such as false perceptions (hallucinations and delusions), manic depressive illness, and severe behavioral problems. It works by interfering with dopaminergic pathways and is highly sedating. The dosage for mild cases is 25 to 50 milligrams; severe cases warrant dosages from 75 to 150 mg. Paige's records further indicate that Thorazine was administered again in December and on through the 19th of April, 1968.

Paige was not mentally ill, so the use of the potent drug Thorazine, with powerful, and occasionally dangerous side effects was an extreme measure. Side effects range from lethargy, sleepiness, or dizziness to more serious conditions such as Tardive dyskinesia, an irreversible neurologic disorder involving uncontrollable movement of various body parts.

What was the rationale for using Thorazine with Paige? Thomas Szasz, who was writing *Ideology and Insanity: Essays on the Psychiatric Dehumanization of Man* in the late sixties, believed that the purpose of psychopharmacology was a desire to control human behavior through chemical agents that either "tranquilized" or "energized." Szasz was most concerned about the "...many persons who do not wish to be drugged - for example, patients committed to mental hospitals and others treated involuntarily - and cannot refuse to be tranquilized into submission." This wise opponent of dehumanizing patients continued:

> *Regardless of the alleged medical-psychiatric merits*
> *of these drugs for the treatment of mental illness,*
> *whenever a person is given such a drug against his*
> *will, it is because those in charge of him wish to alter*
> *his behavior. Whether or not this alteration will*
> *subsequently be considered beneficial by the subject is*
> *another matter. (Szasz, 1970, p.223)*

The most likely motivation for the use of tranquilizing chemical agents by the physicians at Apple Creek, with its 2000 residents, was, in the name of psychiatric therapy, to keep the residents calm and subdued. In other words, as Szasz would say - tranquilized into submission. While Paige remembers exhibiting the usual "youthful exuberance" of a 16 year old, she could not recall any specific misdeeds or behavior patterns that would warrant the use Thorazine to regulate or subdue her behavior.

"I do remember getting very angry about the conditions and the treatment we received in the institution, but it didn't do any good. I guess this [the medication] was their way of helping a person adjust to her surroundings," surmised Paige.

She recalled being in a daze after the Thorazine was administered. "I felt like a zombie because they had me drugged up. I felt like I didn't have any value to anyone and never would."

Soon Paige was subjected to the harsh treatment seemingly reserved for the violent mentally ill. The Ward 11 girls used to play on an outdoor 2nd floor wooden deck, where it was against the rules to run. One day Paige, still as clumsy as she was as a child, fell down while running and badly skinned her knee. Much to her surprise, she was surrounded by two attendants who, instead of bandaging her knee, escorted her to a small room with padded walls. The cubicle was about 5' by 7', with a heavy metal door that had one small window covered with a thick metal mesh. The room contained no furniture or wash stand. This was her punishment for running on the deck: incarceration in a solitary confinement cell where she spent the next two fear-filled days. She was allowed only her meals. Huddled on a bare mattress on the floor, her hours were spent staring up at the single light bulb on the ceiling. A pan was delivered for toileting. At night, when the light bulb went out, she cried softly into the darkness. Never had she been so terrified. Never had she felt so alone.

Even more difficult to fathom were the electroshock treatments. In the late sixties shock was used quite commonly as a treatment for mental illness. Paige claimed that she was taken forcibly into a room with a large operating table in the center. The table was connected to large cables that emerged from beneath the floor. She was placed on the table and strapped down so her arms and legs were immobilized. A cap was strapped onto her head. Then, electric shock was administered through electrodes placed at each side of the head near the temples.

She imagined herself being strapped into an electric chair used to put imprisoned murderers to death, with the only difference being that she was reclining on the table. Thankfully, there was little recollection of the shock. All she would remember is waking up in her own cot - her mind disoriented and her body completely exhausted. The shock treatment was not recorded in Paige's institutional records, although Paige insisted it occurred.

Electroshock therapy delivered electricity by passing 70 to 400 volts with an amperage between 200 and 1600 milliamperes through the brain. So overpowering was the shock that psychiatrists would use electrode jelly to minimize burns to the skin. The hypothesis was that the shock would induce a seizure and thus rearrange the brain chemistry, hopefully for the better. Perhaps because some patients had apparently benefited from shock therapy, many in the medical community speculated that it could help others.

In the introduction to *The History of Shock Treatment* (1978, L. Frank, Ed, p.xiii), Lee Coleman, M.D. discusses how the rationale for electroshock therapy was that the electrical assaults arrange the brain chemistry for the better:

> *Most theorists readily agree, however, that these are speculations; in fact, they seem to take a certain satisfaction in shock treatment's supposedly unknown mode of action... The truth is, however, that electroshock "works" by a mechanism that is simple, straightforward, and understood by many of those who have undergone it and anyone else who truly wanted to find out. Unfortunately, the advocates*

*of electroshock (particularly those who administer
it) refuse to recognize what it does, because to do
so would make them feel bad. Electroshock works
by damaging the brain. Proponents insist that this
damage is negligible and transient - a contention that
is disputed by many who have been subjected to the
procedure. Furthermore, its advocates want to see
this damage as a 'side effect.' In fact, the changes one
sees when electroshock is administered are completely
consistent with any acute brain injury, such as a
blow to the head from a hammer. In essence, what
happens is that the individual is dazed, confused,
and disoriented, and therefore cannot remember or
appreciate current problems.*

We now know that side effects of electroshock treatment are memory loss, diminished intelligence, and brain damage. For Paige, the residue of the unwarranted drugging, isolation, and brutal shock treatments continued to terrorize Paige in her dreams and lingered on in her psyche throughout her life.

Luckily, Apple Creek allowed church services to be conducted. In the first month of admission, back in 1967, Paige was permitted to sing in the choir. The institution staged a beautiful Christmas pageant that first year, and she recollected it as the highlight of that dreadful year. The following February, she was told that she didn't sing well enough to be in the choir. Extremely disappointed, Paige found her only consolation in being permitted to continue her music class. Her hold on normality in the insane world of the institution was strengthened by nondenominational church services, which she attended regularly.

"I knew there was a God," she recalled, "but where was He? I was lonely, angry, and confused in Apple Creek. I missed my family and friends and I was so scared that I would never get out. It was a desolate time in my life."

> *When I first came to Apple Creek, I was convinced*
> *that I didn't belong in the institution, but as time*
> *went on, I began to doubt myself. I actually started*
> *to believe that I did belong there, even though I*
> *wasn't like everyone else.*

Paradoxically, wrenchingly so, even the horrors of Apple Creek presented opportunities for Paige's growth, learning, and fulfillment. While confined, Paige was taught some important skills. She learned domestic ones from the aides, who insisted that she always be neat and clean. In Ward 11, she had to meticulously fold her clothes in her drawers in order to make "Honor Roll" status.

According to Paige, "You had to do things just right, and a pair of dirty underwear in your drawers could cost you points. I didn't get away with any sloppiness!"

If a patient earned a certain number of points, she could go to the Wednesday night dance or the Saturday night movie. Paige was very neat and clean. The domestic skills shaped at Apple Creek along with the caregiving expertise gained as a Patient Aide were useful in attaining numerous jobs and satisfactory living situations since her release.

There were also some lighthearted moments at Apple Creek which Paige later shared with her friend and supervisor Dick Tryon:

> *Paige told numerous stories about her years in institu-*
> *tions. Her favorites were about the "Three Muske-*
> *teers" - two other residents and herself - who often*
> *played pranks. Once they set all of the clocks in their*
> *unit ahead by an hour. The staff started leaving ear-*
> *ly until someone noticed that the next shift had not*
> *come on yet. Another incident was when the "Three*
> *Musketeers" hid in the back seat of the car belonging*
> *to their favorite staff person. When she had driven*
> *out of the institution, the three girls jumped up yell-*
> *ing "Surprise!" Paige thought this might have been a*
> *bad idea, because the staff person wet herself.*

"There were some very kind and caring nurses and aides at Apple
Creek," recollected Paige. "They even remembered me after 27 years!"[2]

Overall, though, Paige's experience at Apple Creek was like a bad
dream that wouldn't disappear, repeating itself day after day. "Every day
was the same. I saw absolutely no future for me - I didn't look forward,
I didn't look back. The place was a madhouse."

In the institutional madhouse, in near suspended animation, Paige
discovered what it feels like to be rejected by family and society. She
learned how it feels to be forced to live and learn apart from the larger

2: Today, Apple Creek is no longer the same institution. It has evolved into a smaller
Developmental Center with completely different policies and attitudes aimed at promoting quality of life and the transition to more independent living for its consumers
with disabilities.

community. It was the beginning of a nightmare which was to recur in several more facilities.

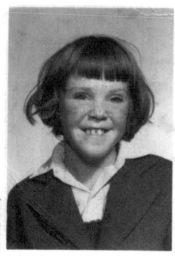

Paige in elementary school, age 9

Paige's admission photo at
Apple Creek State Hospital
October 10, 1967, age 15

Paige (2nd from left)
as a patient aide at Apple
Creek State Hospital

McIntosh Building,
Apple Creek State
Hospital

Chapter 6

I'll Fly Away

*One can never consent to creep when one feels the
impulse to soar.*

-Helen Keller

Certain moments of our lives loom large in our memories. Even relatively short periods merely spanning a mere few years, or even months,
can mold our development in crucial ways. Paige's confinement at
Apple Creek State Mental Hospital altered the course of her life so
dramatically that the two and a half years she was a enrolled there were
formative in her developing mind and personality.

As a rule, the only time Paige was permitted to leave the grounds of
Apple Creek was for Christmas vacation with her family. She remembered these holidays as the highlights of her otherwise grim incarceration at Apple Creek. The time she spent with her brothers and sisters
was precious to her, and she detested having to return to the confines
of the institution.

In 1969, Ms. Barton also had misgivings about Paige's returning to
Apple Creek. After Christmas vacation that year, she wrote the institution's social worker requesting a placement closer to home. Ms. Barton
suggested that Paige attend Madison Opportunity Village (MOV), a
residential facility for "the mentally retarded." Referring to MOV as a
"pleasant place," - especially when compared to the deplorable environ-

ment of Apple Creek State Mental Hospital - Paige's mother hoped that she "could be trained for some minimal job," or learn some "handi-work with her friends." It was evident that no such training or education was offered at Apple Creek, as was anticipated when the Bartons first enrolled Paige. The family wanted Paige to remain at home until closer accommodations could be found. "She is happy here and, as I said, we are enjoying her stay," wrote Ms. Barton.

After conferring with the social worker from Madison Opportunity Village, she formally requested to the Superintendent at Apple Creek that Paige be transferred to Madison Opportunity Village. The Super-intendent's reply, dated February 27, 1970, stated his frank opinion that Paige was not a good candidate for Madison Opportunity Village, however he indicated that she could be evaluated for a limited period of time - one or two months. After which, she should either return home or to the hospital. His letter closed with his honest opinion:

> *Frankly, [I] prefer to have her go back home as we*
> *have nothing to offer here and she is not eligible for*
> *our services by any stretch of the imagination.*

Superintendent Stover's memo left no doubt that he and his staff believed Paige was misplaced in the state mental hospital.

Heidi

Paige's sister Heidi visited her at Apple Creek, sometimes bringing her younger brothers and sisters, Robin, Holly, and Gene, with her. Born in 1950, sister Heidi was a year older than Paige. When Heidi was four years old, she was diagnosed with severe juvenile diabetes, also referred to as type 1 diabetes, which results in an excess of glucose in the blood. Type 1 diabetes is caused by damage to the pancreas and the beta cells that produce insulin. Insulin is the polypeptide hormone responsible for transporting the glucose from the blood and delivering it to the billions of cells in the body. High glucose levels in the blood can damage the eyes, kidneys, nerves, and heart.

During the time when Paige was at Apple Creek, Heidi had been plagued by the debilitating effects of diabetes, including severe insulin reactions involving convulsions and even unconsciousness. After Heidi graduated from high school, she attended Ohio State University at the same time Paige was at Apple Creek. Paige remembers that at that time Heidi's health was deteriorating fairly rapidly. When she had been living at home, Heidi was able to control her diet and medication regimen, perhaps because her parents kept a watchful eye on her. But college life was wild in the late '60s and '70s - especially at Ohio State - where the social life was dominated by parties and drinking.

"Like a kid, Heidi would get loose, eat candy, drink, and take more insulin," according to Paige. "These were dangerous behaviors for a diabetic," reminisced Paige, who was highly familiar with the effects and treatment of diabetes, inasmuch as she had type 2 diabetes. Unlike type 1, type 2 diabetes is non-insulin dependent, which in Paige's case occurred gradually over time during adulthood. Fortunately, Paige's production of insulin was only slightly below normal, so she was able to control her disease through dietary moderation. In contrast, Heidi's diabetes required insulin injections, a strict diet, and careful monitoring of her blood sugar levels.

Heidi majored in social work at Ohio State. According to Paige, "She was becoming a social worker in order to get people like me out of institutions and into productive lives." At the time, Heidi actively pursued Paige's release from Apple Creek. "She was trying to help me get out, but she wasn't having much luck. I was told that if I wanted out, I had to go to a foster home or a group home, " Paige reported.

Both Heidi and Paige knew that a foster home would be a better alternative than her present hellish institutional home. In the fall of 1969, one of the Apple Creek social workers located a foster home in Mansfield, Ohio, about 30 miles from Apple Creek. It was referred to as the "Kilgore Home," according to institutional records. Paige's memories of her Kilgore Home foster placement were ambivalent: happy to enjoy a measure of freedom but cognizant that her new placement was no utopia.

> *My mother did not know about my release [to the foster home] until later. I liked it there, but I was used to keeping busy in the past and was bored with not enough to do. It was so nice to be out in the world again - I had really forgotten what it was like! All the other girls that were in the foster home worked at a sheltered workshop, but my I.Q. was too high for me to be allowed to work there.*

> *While I was at the Kilgore Home, one of the residents stole my wallet which had all the money I had to my name. They spent every cent. I didn't know what to do to get my money back.*

Indeed, Ms. Barton initially wasn't aware of the foster placement,

but she ultimately found out. Once she learned that Paige was at
the Kilgore Home, she paid a visit. She vividly recalls an image of 7
young men and women sitting aimlessly, without direction, on long
wooden benches for hours and hours. Her estimation of the sheltered
workshop was that it was deplorable, and she was adamantly opposed
to Paige ever working there. Sheltered workshops were - and still are
- segregated community-based work facilities for people with moderate
and severe disabilities. While the purpose of publicly funded sheltered
workshops was to educate and train adults with developmental disabilities for gainful employment, in reality, the "workers" often passed their
time in mindless production tasks, such as sorting plastic utensils or
assembling "widgets." Unfortunately, such make-work tasks have little
similarity to the type of work available in actual community employment settings. While it is true that the production work might have
served a therapeutic purpose of keeping the clients engaged during
the day, it did not contribute substantially to their growth and development. Ms. Barton was correct in her estimation that the sheltered
workshop was a demeaning "simulated" work setting and that the work
activities would have little relevance to Paige's future employment possibilities.

After Paige's short stint at the Kilgore foster home, she returned to her
family's home at North Madison for Christmas and stayed on until she
entered the Madison Opportunity Village the following September.
Ms. Barton remembers the fall of 1970, because the family erroneously received a bill for $10,000.00 to cover Paige's residential costs.
Technically, she was still a ward of the state and on the "state roll," and
the matter was resolved after the Bartons contacted the Ohio Attorney
General's Office. The charges were waived.

Madison Opportunity Village, or MOV, as it was sometimes called, was a community residential facility that offered training for jobs and independent living skills. Independent living skills were designated as those needed to adjust to life in the community, such as domestic skills (laundering, household cleaning), self-help skills (dressing, eating, and toileting), interpersonal skills, and consumer skills (money management, budgeting). The Madison Opportunity Village facility was a large brick building much like the gloomy hospital building at Apple Creek. There were two wings to the facility, one for elderly women and another for younger ones. This time Paige lived on Ward 101, which was much like Apple Creek, according to Paige, only not as large nor nearly as confining. Like Apple Creek, residents were granted little privacy, as two or three people shared the rooms. The routine was much like an institution's - rigid and monotonous. The staff exercised similar control over the residents - telling them when to wake up, when to eat, when to sleep, and even when to brush their teeth. Essentially, Paige had moved from one institution to another, only MOV was nominally a "community institution," though communal camaraderie came in small doses.

Paige recalls the training she received in domestic skills. "They taught us to clean, and we washed the floors on our hands and knees." Of course, the training was not compensated. Like Apple Creek, MOV practiced peonage in the name of training. Paige wondered whether she were fated to become a domestic worker someday, deploring the thought of cleaning and washing for the rest of her life. Her premonition turned out to be partially accurate, and the training would come in handy in one of her first "real" jobs in the community.

While at MOV, Paige became a Nurse's Aide for the Gabel's Nursing

Home, a medical facility that housed children with mental retardation. "I only made a dollar an hour at the nursing home," says Paige. "Not exactly minimum wage, but it was good job training." Ironically, her near drudgery as a Patient Aide at Apple Creek proved to be advantageous in preparing her for work at the nursing home.

It was hard for Paige to put into words how momentous the newfound freedom of being allowed to walk independently to and from work was. Most Americans, who, accustomed to a semi-sedentary lifestyle, depend on their cars to transport them to work even when their work is less than a mile away, would consider walking an annoyance. Walking slows us down, taking precious moments from the rush of our fast-paced lives. But to Paige, it was as though she was a caged bird who had discovered the door to the cage was open. She felt her wings unfolding and was soon flying from captivity. She breathed in the freedom with the sweet fragrance of the pines: Independence like a current of wind carried her effortlessly through the sky. Regaining a liberty lost since her public school days, her spirit was transported. Never again would she take for granted the simple joy of strolling to and from work on her own.

Meanwhile, Heidi's diabetic condition was steadily worsening. The previous February, she had lost her sight, and she was unable to put her degree in social work to use. Discouraged and gravely ill, she returned home to live in the care of her family.

According to the Nursing Notes, observations recorded on the residents at the Opportunity Village, on May 10, 1973, Paige returned from her job at the Gable's home "crying very hard." When asked what was wrong, she stated, "My sister is in a coma, and Dad worried that she wouldn't live." The nurse reported that she tried to talk to Paige and that she stopped crying, but that she was "very nervous." The next morning Paige was "more settled and played the organ."

Paige called to mind the delightful time that summer when Heidi brought a beautiful little yellow lab puppy home with her. It was meant to become her seeing-eye dog. Sadly, Heidi was unable to keep the dog because in July she was hospitalized. Her condition worsened, and in September she was moved to another hospital in Columbus where she remained until December.

The morning of December 10th, 1973 was engraved in Paige's memory. She was working at the Gables Nursing Home and had been living at home since summertime. At 5:30 am, her parents had gone to the hospital for an emergency. Her mother had called from the hospital to tell Paige to go to work.

Paige was at work when she had a foreboding instinct, knowing that something was terribly wrong, but unsure of what it was. She remembered that it was exactly 11:00 am when a staff member told her that Heidi had died. Not knowing what to do, she continued working that day.

That evening, in shock from the news, Paige collected all the stuffed frogs she could find, because Heidi loved frogs. She lovingly placed one in the coffin at the funeral wake. Paige did not attend calling hours, because it was decided that she couldn't handle the strain. "They didn't want me to cry. They didn't want me to make a scene," asserted Paige, somewhat resentfully.

*I will never forget how I felt the day Heidi died. It
just didn't seem fair that someone so young and so
full of potential had died. That day I made myself a
promise that some time in the future I would fulfill
Heidi's wishes and free myself from institutional life.*

It was Heidi who always had faith in Paige. And it was Heidi who
inculcated in Paige the courage to persevere even in desperate circumstances. Heidi's blend of perfection and imperfection, her saintly and
wild ways, and her constant belief in Paige served as a lifetime inspiration. Paige would keep the vow she made to Heidi.

Lake County Mental Retardation Center

That same year, 1973, Paige worked for a while in her mother's card
shop. She also attended social functions at a facility called the Lake
County Mental Retardation Center in Mentor, Ohio. She liked what
she saw there.

*They helped people get jobs and taught them how to
live on their own. I applied, without my mother's
knowledge, and was accepted. When the acceptance
came in the mail she agreed and took me there to
live. I really liked it there. We had a lot more freedom than I had at the other institutions. We were
allowed to go to the mall for shopping and we could
do whatever we wanted in the evenings.*

Even though the facility in Mentor was residential and was designed for
people with mental retardation - which we know Paige did not have - it

contributed to her development by preparing her to live on the outside. For most of the late sixties and seventies, Paige had lived almost exclusively in segregated settings for people with mental illness, mental retardation, or physical disabilities. "At least," rationalized Paige, "the Lake County MR Center was a step up from a total-care institution to a partial-care one." Paige was definitely allowed more freedom there, such as being able to go to the shopping mall or choose what she wanted to do in the evenings. But she still had to conform to the regimen and lack of privacy associated with institutional life. She acknowledged that it was their job, but she was piqued by the violation of her privacy and dignity when staff members observed clients showering. They even kept records on tooth brushing. But, on the whole, Paige felt that Lake County MR Center was essential in preparing her to transition from the bizarre world of institutions to the community.

Erving Goffman, in his book *Asylums* (1961), stated that institutions, by their nature, were self-corrupting. Initially, the professionals and staff determine that the "patient" is ill (mentally ill or mentally retarded), and they map out what the patient must do to recover from the illness. The oppressor first subjugates his or her patient and then cites the patient's oppressed status as proof of his own inferiority. Patients are stripped of their legal rights, imprisoned without a trial, and then subjected to unspeakable tyranny and degradation - concealed, of course, from the public eye.

While Paige was undergoing training in domestic skills, she encountered frightening and repulsive degradation by an authority figure. A Mental Retardation (MR) Counselor used the work situation to sexually abuse his clients, namely Paige and two other women. The three young women were taken to the MR Counselor's home, supposedly to learn domestic skills by cleaning his house. While the four of them were alone in his home, the supervisor would take each woman upstairs into the bedroom - one at a time. What happened in the bedroom would have resulted in a criminal proceeding today. "I was scared to death," said Paige. "I knew it was wrong, and yet I had no power to stop it."

Eventually, one of the women, Geraldine, had the courage to divulge the supervisor's sexually predatory behavior to another staff member at Lake County. "Before I knew it, they had moved Geraldine out. Gone. I never saw her again," recalled Paige. "When my mom found out, she was irate. The counselor was fired. Luckily, by the time he was exposed, I'd landed a job as a housekeeping aide at a nursing home so nothing happened to me. But my friend wasn't so lucky." Paige later said that this had been her only experience with sex and it forever tainted her, warping her perspective on intimate relationships. She could not contemplate a sexual relationship without feeling the fear and shame aroused by the ghosts of sexual victimization.

These young women should never have been subjected to this humiliation. Yet they were. Sexual abuse was certainly not unheard of in institutions and community facilities for people with disabilities. The "patients" are vulnerable, often incapable of expressing what has happened to them. The opportunities for abuse, whether sexual, physical, or emotional, are facilitated by the "patients'" segregation from the watchful, caring eyes of the families and the community.

As Paige continued to explore job possibilities in the community, she found it increasingly apparent that landing a good job would require a high school diploma. Her formal education ceased when she left

Redbird Middle School, and her years spent in institutions were a total loss educationally. Indeed, if institutions were incapable of offering residents humane care, it is logical that they were much less able and willing to provide educational opportunities and training for work.

When institutions were first established in the early 1900's in the US, their purpose was to afford their residents a decent education. However, when they became overcrowded and squeezed in the fifties and sixties, they simply served as custodial facilities, forsaking their educative function. It wasn't until 1975, when Congress passed the Education for All Handicapped Children Act, PL 94-142, that institutions were legally required to educate residents who were of school age.

Paige accepted the fact that she had missed out on a high school education, and she knew she was too old to go back to school at age 28. Nonetheless, a goal was solidifying in her mind: obtaining a high school diploma. Paige's ability to let go of the past, to release bitterness and anger, and to move forward in attaining her goals was essential to passing the threshold of opportunity. Positively focusing on future goals is a key to success that many have yet to learn, but which Paige had mastered. It would have been so easy for her to be embittered and consumed with the mistreatment and deprivation she experienced in institutions. But self-pity was not her style, and it would have diverted her from what she most wanted in life: an education, a job, and a life in the community.

In her characteristically tenacious manner, Paige decided that she would complete her General Education Diploma, or GED, on her own. Another strategy Paige used to great advantage throughout her adult life was seeking help from others when she needed it. She knew that she had to identify individuals who could direct her and secure for her the requisite materials, applications, books, or whatever else she needed. She learned that shyness would have diminished her possibilities. Paige was anything but reserved and withdrawn, and it is hard to imagine that she could have overcome the formidable barriers posed by a lack of education and a history of institutionalization if she had allowed herself to shrink into a shell of reclusivity or timidity. Her progress depended on her ability to reach out to others for assistance, which may explain her sometimes pushy, overly gregarious, and obtrusive behavior. These behaviors were survival skills, not lack of refinement. Seeking a social worker at Lake County, she asked for assistance in finding the books to study for the GED exam. But she was disappointed with the social worker's naysaying.

"You can't be serious! You'll never pass the GED because you haven't had any high school background."

Paige's reply was "But I have to try. I don't know if I will pass, but I have to try."

Paige obtained the books she needed and studied for two years. One of the guidance counselors helped when she could. Much to everyone's surprise, Paige passed all the tests and was awarded her high school equivalency diploma in June, 1979. She had been convinced that with hard work she could pass the exam. Unfortunately, she herself seemed to be the only one with faith that Paige Barton could prevail. Attaining her GED was a major milestone for Paige, certainly her most important accomplishment while residing at Lake County MR Center. Paige was cognizant that passing the GED exam was only a single step in her life's journey, but it was an essential one imperative for further education.

Later that year, Paige was tested at Lake County MR Center to determine her intellectual capabilities. She took an IQ test which established, again, that she did not have mental retardation. This time her IQ score fell in the average range. In Paige's words: "They looked at my score and said 'You have to get out of here.'" Her reply was "Teach me how to live on the outside, and I'll go."

There is a saying that you cannot fly like an eagle with the wings of a wren. Paige needed training.

> *I remained in the center until the summer of 1980.*
> *They helped me a lot by preparing me to move out on*
> *my own and helping me get a job. I was working at*
> *a nursing home as a housekeeping aide.*
>
> *When I first moved out of the center I moved in with*
> *an elderly lady. I was considered to be in her care.*
> *She was able to be by herself during the day when*
> *I worked at the nursing home, but that changed*
> *quickly. In the fall of 1980, her condition got worse*
> *and they put her into a nursing home. It was then*
> *that I decided to move to Maine, where my brother*
> *lived.*

Paige knew she would have to make some changes when she left Lake County. While living at the various segregated facilities, she had learned to behave in ways that were common in those settings, but would not be permissible or even agreeable in the community. For example, everyone swore in the institutions - and Paige had developed quite a repertoire of foul words that were an integral part of her working vocabulary.

"I spent my days with people who would only listen if you swore at them, so that is what I did," she explained.

Another unbecoming habit Paige failed to overcome during adolescence and adulthood was thumb sucking. A childish behavior that should have faded away decades earlier, thumb sucking seemed to provide Paige with comfort and security. She started smoking in her twenties, which replaced the need to suck her thumb with a more dangerous habit (as it does for many people, even though they won't admit it). When she quit smoking in her thirties, her thumb would sometimes wend its way to her mouth, even in professional meetings and public settings. Try as she might, thumb sucking was a habit that she never quite overcame. It was evident that it embarrassed her when others discovered her babyish behavior. But learning to forgive herself for reverting to childish habits helped her survive the terrifying nightmare of institutionalization. Bad habits sometimes serve purposes that are essential to one's survival.

In the seventies and eighties, the public policy of deinstitutionalization, or moving people out of large residential facilities and into smaller, more homelike facilities in the community, was enjoying widespread advocacy. Underlying the deinstitutionalization movement was the philosophical principle of normalization, originating in Scandinavia in the 1960's and articulated by N.E. Bank-Mikkelsen and Bengt Nirje in 1969 and further described by Wolf Wolfensberger in the US in the early 1970's. By definition, the concept of normalization meant that all people, including those with developmental disabilities, would share:

Patterns of life and conditions of everyday living,
which are as close as possible to the regular circum-
stances and ways of life of society...a normal rhythm
of the day, with privacy, activities and mutual
responsibility; a normal rhythm of the week, with a
home to live in, a school or work to go to, and leisure
time with a modicum of social interaction; a nor-
mal rhythm of the year...opportunity to undergo the
normal developmental experiences of the life cycle...
respect and understanding given to the silent wishes
or expressed self-determination...relationships be-
tween sexes... If retarded persons cannot or should not
live in their family or own home, the homes provided
should be of normal size and situated in normal
residential areas. (Nirje, 1976, pp.231-232)

The normalization principle described goals and standards of treatment
to guide the processes of services for people with mental retardation
and developmental disabilities who had historically been devalued by
society. Normalization, as a cultural and moral conviction, was incom-
patible with institutionalization. After all, institutions did not provide
residents a lifestyle that was culturally normative - the essential ingredient of normalization.

In the early seventies, a court case, Wyatt v. Stickney (1972), stressed
the importance of community-based training for residents of institutions. In part, the opinion read:

Residents shall have a right to the least restrictive
conditions necessary to achieve the purposes of habilitation.
To this end, the institution shall make every attempt to

> *move residents from:*
> > *(a) more to less structured living;*
> > *(b) larger to smaller facilities;*
> > *(c) larger to smaller living units;*
> > *(d) group to individual residence;*
> > *(e) segregated from the community to integrated*
> > > *into the community;*
> > *(f) dependent to independent living (p. 396).*

The Wyatt court decreed it was no longer justifiable for institutions to function as warehouses to remove people with mental retardation from society. Residential facilities were now responsible for habilitating the residents, or providing training and services that foster the ability to flourish in community living as well as assuring "safety and freedom from undue restraint" (Lakin & Bruininks, 1985).

The era of the seventies introduced a crusade for institutional reform, and by the end of the decade, the reform movement attempted to propel residents out of the overcrowded and depersonalized institutions into smaller, less restrictive, community based facilities. However, depopulating institutions wasn't always effected in the most supportive ways or with the best interests of the residents in mind. In the case of Lake County MR Center, residents were randomly farmed out into communities where they saw no friends, no family, no familiar faces. Sometimes they were placed in isolated apartments by themselves. In many cases, the transition was too abrupt, and the rush to deinstitutionalize created serious adjustment problems in the community.

The necessity of preparation to live outside the walls of the institution was underscored in the untimely death of one of Paige's friends from the Lake County MR Center named Doris. Doris was being released from Lake County to live in her own apartment in the city of Cleveland.

"The last I heard of Doris was that she made the mistake of inviting a stranger into her apartment, and that she was murdered," Paige recalls. "At age 46, after 23 years of institutional living, they threw her into the community," says Paige with a hint of anger in her voice. "But we all knew she wasn't ready. It was frightening." Sadly enough, sometimes the result of poorly planned deinstitutionalization was homelessness or a senseless tragedy such as Doris'.

It was about this time when Paige was struggling with existing on the outside. Some friends said that they knew of something that could help: they invited her to a church service at the Church of God. Though the service differed from her past religious experiences, she found it moving. The women at the church told her that she should come back the next week if she wanted to give her heart to the Lord.

"Why? What's wrong with me that I need to give my heart to the Lord?" inquired Paige.

They responded, "Well, you have a filthy mouth, you cuss, you're lost." They also told her that whenever they needed something, they would pray, "and there it was."

With reservations, Paige reluctantly decided to return to the church the next Sunday, and as Paige put it, "When they made the altar call and gave the salvation message, I jumped over people's feet to get to the altar. Something very special happened to me that day: I accepted Jesus as my Savior." Almost immediately, her swearing subsided, and after smoking for more than ten years, she instantly gave it up.   It was easy.

> *In 1980 I moved to Maine because my parents and brother had moved there while I was living in the various institutions. Most of all, I wanted to be closer to my family. No more institutions, no group homes, no foster homes - I just wanted to live a normal life. I wanted to have a normal job with a normal income.*
>
> *Even though my parents thought I should move closer to them in Kennebunkport, I chose to live near my brother, Peter, who was further north in the town of Pittsfield. I knew that if I moved back home, they would just find another place to put me in. And that was the last thing I wanted in my life.*

Paige lived temporarily with Peter in Pittsfield for about a month, and then she found a job in the town of Skowhegan. She was a live-in houskeeper for a retired dentist who owned a stately New England home, overlooking the Kennebec River. Paige loved the hardwood floors, the polished wood furniture, and the sparkling glass windows that framed beautiful vistas of the river.

The Kennebec River and the town of Skowhegan are symbolic of a vibrant relationship between the land of Maine and its people. The dam and old mill form the center of town, with the quiet waters of the impoundment reaching upriver to Norridgewock. Below the dam all the pent-up energy of the mighty Kennebec is released in a frothing torrent that roars between parallel bedrock cliffs with undaunted energy and undeterred resolve. Perhaps, as she gazed down upon the exuberant river as it escaped its bondage, Paige identified with the parallel of her own life, as her life force burst free from the fetters of institutional incarceration.

The elegance of her new home was completely unlike her destitute and sterile living quarters in the institutions. She gladly cleaned his house and cooked meals for this gentleman for three years, until he became too ill to live at home.

Having met her goal of gainful employment, albeit at minimum wage, she dared to dream even more.

If I could get a college education, I could work with young children with disabilities, thought Paige.

But Paige's desire for a college education wasn't solely related to entering the workforce. Paige wanted to become a more learned person. She wanted to explore the world of ideas, the world of the arts. She wanted to encounter others with these interests. And, like many prospective college students, she wanted to be free and have some fun.

Chapter 7

Intersections

If you think education is expensive, try ignorance.
-Derek Bok

In 1983, after the Skowhegan dentist Paige worked for moved into a nursing home, she needed to search for a new job. She decided to enroll in a course to become a Certified Nurse's Assistant, in hopes that she could find a job in a nursing home or health care facility.

> *I was having a tough time finding a job in Skow-hegan, so I started thinking I would look for work at Farmington. Also, my brother Peter had moved from Pittsfield to Strong, which was only about 20 minutes away from Farmington. So I went to Farmington and applied for work, but no one seemed to be hiring. I kept praying and God helped me get a job at Sandy River Nursing Care Center as a housekeeping aide in September 1983.*

The Sandy River Nursing Home was several miles from Farmington at the foot of the mountains. Near the University of Maine at Farmington, Paige found a duplex that she shared with an elderly woman. In return for a portion of the rent, she helped her housemate with minor chores. She now had a job and a place to live. The next step was to investigate whether she could somehow get into college.

First, she had to prove to the admissions officers at the university that she was serious and that they should take a chance on her. Just before the start of classes in September, 1984, Paige met with one of the admissions officers at the university. With only a GED and no high school education, she seemed unlikely to be competitive with the other freshmen applicants. The university was small, accepting about five hundred new students each year in order to keep the total enrollment at 2,000. Fortunately, the Director of Admissions, Jim Collins, was a caring man who encouraged Paige to take some courses as a non-degree seeking student.

"If you do well," he told her, "you'll have a better chance at being admitted to a degree program."

This plan sounded intelligent to Paige, and she signed up for the freshman English composition course, Eng 101. Having missed out on high school classes or any formal college courses, she had no idea whether she would succeed in college. But, indomitably, she thought, how would she know if she didn't try?

She wanted a chance to take one course - to find out whether she could hold her own at the university level. The admissions office extended to her a golden opportunity, and she pledged to herself that she would not waste it. Mr. Collins cracked opened the door to a very important and formative period that would ultimately redirect the course of her life. She knew that the University of Maine at Farmington (UMF) was right for her - comprised of a supportive and caring community that was willing to venture a chance on her abilities.

Although Paige was fully aware of the huge personal and financial responsibility to which she was committing, not for one moment did she doubt her decision to enter the university. She was determined to prove herself academically; she would not squander this wondrous possibility. Recognizing the major gaps in her own education, she resolved to do whatever was necessary to succeed. She knew it would take extraordinary focus and hard work. As was her style, she thought carefully about what she wanted and how she was going to go about obtaining her goal, and, then, in Paige's words, to "GO FOR IT!" with everything she had. Her single-mindedness surfaced at this crucial point.

Paige's mother disagreed with her choice to enroll in college. She worried that even with a college degree, Paige would land only the kinds of jobs which would not justify the enormous expense of college.

"I can't say I was in favor of college. For one thing, it was hideously expensive. But she was determined! And nothing was going to stop her," said Ms. Barton.

Success breeds success, and having first obtained her GED and then having corralled several jobs, albeit only a cut above menial ones, Paige had made enough headway to whet her appetite for new challenges. Knowing that her mother, family, and friends disapproved of her decision only strengthened her will to prevail and aroused Paige's ambitions all the more.

To Paige, the disturbing paradox was that her family esteemed higher education - yet they couldn't seem to understand why she should be entitled to similar aspirations. Her siblings had gone to college, some to very prestigious universities such as Drexel, Pennsylvania State University, and Harvard. Ms. Barton had graduated from Wellesley, the highly regarded women's college in Massachusetts.

Her family's negativity reinforced the feelings of inferiority Paige had lived with all her life. Everyone else could go to college, but Paige wasn't worthy of an education. Paige's reaction to the rationale that college was "hideously expensive" was to be contrary. Furthermore, she truly believed that a college education was the way out of her financial and social poverty.

No matter if others lacked confidence in her, their naysaying simply hardened Paige's resolve. Her constant motto was, *Tell me I can't do something, then stand by and watch me try!*

But Ms. Barton was correct in recognizing that college was expensive and that Paige would find financing an education to be a major hurdle. Working as a Certified Nurse's Assistant hardly paid enough to make ends meet, a minimum wage of about $500 a month. Even combined with an additional housekeeping job, she would never be able to afford college. The tuition alone was several thousand a semester. Books were also expensive, many costing over $50.

Paige had accepted the fact that she would not receive support from her family to cover college costs. But the saying is that "the Lord works in mysterious ways," and no one, including Paige, could have imagined how she would ultimately chance upon the money for school.

On a Saturday afternoon in February, 1984, Paige was on her way home from doing her laundry at the local laundromat. Main Street was the archetype of a winter image of a traditional western Maine town. The picturesque brick buildings were artistically draped with a blanket of clean snow. More snow, a little grimy, was mounded high between the street and sidewalk, obscuring the view and sound of the sparse traffic. The few people out on foot walked carefully on the icy paths, using the characteristic northern gait of small, short steps to keep the weight centered over a securely placed foot, with eyes focused down to choose the next. One recognized an acquaintance by his or her characteristic clothing, as hats and scarves concealed all physical features, along with the peripheral vision and hearing of the wearer.

With the full laundry basket in her hands, Paige stepped into the street at the crosswalk across from Merrill Bank. Plodding a few feet into the street, Paige saw a towel fall from the basket. Stooping down to pick it up, she didn't notice that the light had changed. The next thing she knew, she was in the hospital, having been struck by a pick-up truck that was moving through the intersection.

> *Luckily the wheels of the truck didn't run over me. I was actually hit by the snow plow on the front of the truck. I managed to survive with only bumps and bruises and a cut on the inside of my mouth. God once more was watching out for me. I came very close to not living to tell the tale.*

In addition to the charming new dimple in Paige's left cheek, the accident resulted in a settlement of $5,000 that Paige would use toward her education, her medications, and her living expenses. Shortly after the accident, she had been advised to see an attorney about recovering some of her medical expenses. In the process of investigating the situation, the attorney interviewed family members and examined Paige's medical records. Not realizing that Paige had never been told about her diagnosis, he innocently said, "Your brother told me that you have Down syndrome."

Paige was almost too stunned to speak. She was struck by the casualness of the comment, juxtaposed with the enormity of its implications.

"That was the first time I had ever heard those words. I didn't know what they meant. I went to the nursing home and asked one of the nurses to explain it to me," she recalled.

Although initially she was shocked, after thinking about it, her reaction was mixed. On one hand, she was relieved to know, finally, what was wrong with her. The label explained why she had always been treated differently, why she was sent away from home, and even why she had problems with her hearing and lungs. On the other hand, she felt angry about never having been told.

"How could my entire family have known all those years without telling me? Why was I the last one to find out?" questioned Paige. "Maybe knowing would have helped me deal with the kids at school who were picking on me. Maybe I would have understood why I was sent away to the institution."

One of the nurses at the Sandy River Nursing Home, who happened to be the daughter of a geneticist Paige would meet a few years in the future, was able to provide a textbook description of Down syndrome.

Paige knew that people with Down syndrome were usually retarded or mentally delayed, so it was devastating to think that she, too, might be retarded. She wondered why the term "mongoloid" also appeared in her records. It was understandable that the chromosomal disorder Trisomy 21 was named for John Langdon Down, the man who discovered the syndrome - but what was the origin of the term mongoloid? Why not "oriental," or "Asian," if the collection of symptoms were similar to the physical appearance of people from Asia?

The Mongols were actually nomadic horsemen who in the thirteenth century conquered the known world. Incredibly fierce and innovative warriors, the Mongol Horde was greatly feared by Western enemies. Indeed, the whole of Western Europe was in imminent danger of falling to the Mongols as previously had Russia, Hungary, the Balkans, and Austria, at the time of its potentate Genghis Khan's death in 1227. They were so feared and loathed in Europe that parents threatened their children with the "Tartars" (Mongols) to make them behave. Western culture perpetuated the view of the expansionist Mongols as frightening, barbaric, brutal and repulsive. Although the supposedly merciless Mongol armies killed enormous numbers of people, they behaved no worse than did invaders from any other culture of that time, they were just more successful. Thus, linking physical attributes and the label "Mongoloid" or "Mongolian Idiot" carried derogatory inferences that are deeply rooted in Western culture.

Interestingly, Genghis Khan is still revered by the Mongol people as the bravest and greatest leader who ever lived. As a young orphan whose chieftain father had been assassinated, he was a hunted fugitive, alone in the world. Through his own initiative and resourcefulness, he unified the nomadic tribes of the steppes and conquered the world, from

China to Russia, the Middle East and Eastern Europe. He initiated religious freedom and believed that a person should achieve status through merit, not on the basis of race or religion. During the period of Genghis Khans' leadership, the Mongols were unstoppable. Perhaps Paige would have secretly approved of the label - now applied as an insult, but also suggestive of the noble qualities and resolve through which the superb Mongol force gained world dominion.

Sadly, the use of the term "mongoloid" in the 1960s and 1970s really boiled down to creating negative, erroneous stereotypes of children who were considered hopelessly retarded. Even today, libraries still house research articles and textbooks from the 1960s that used the pejorative label "Mongolian Idiot."

The pickup accident only served to increase Ms. Barton's misgivings about Paige's ability to live independently in the community. Her mother lacked confidence that Paige could sensibly manage her money, her diet, and life on her own. It would be better, she believed, for Paige to get a job and support herself. In her opinion, someone needed to attend to Paige's welfare and oversee her affairs before something more serious happened to her. Given Heidi's diabetes and her questionable dietary habits in college that preceded her death, it is understandable that Ms. Barton would be similarly concerned about Paige, who also was a diabetic.

Paige's first semester of college entailed taking only one English course, so the cost was affordable. That semester flew by, and Paige earned a B plus in the course - a respectable low honors grade in anyone's first college course by any standards, especially since many students often find freshman English their nemesis. That fall Paige had earned the right to proceed into the Early Childhood Education Associate's Degree Program for the following spring semester. She was absolutely thrilled.

The second semester wasn't as easy. Taking three courses turned out to be exponentially more difficult than taking one. Juggling work and school was demanding. And the breadth of the material in comprehensive introductory courses made it particularly difficult given Paige's limited experiential and knowledge base. She was practically devoid of the foundational knowledge most students gain in high school.

"General Psychology was a bear! I completely failed it that semester," said Paige. Repeating the course, even with tutoring, didn't help. She managed to fail general psychology two more times before she graduated. However, her performance in Psy 230, Death and Dying, was quite commendable, as testified by her A. The course helped her cope with her sister Heidi's death. Years later it would also help ease the ache and suffering she felt over the deaths of young children with Trisomy 18 and 13 - the premature deaths that make one question God's goodness and mercy . . .

Paige's assignment in the course was to write a letter to her deceased sister Heidi.

> *I remember asking the professor, 'How do I deal with Heidi's death when she died so many years ago?' She told me to write a letter. It seemed silly, but I did what she told me. She liked my letter so much that she kept it. A couple of years later she asked me to come to one of her classes. There was a woman there with a grandchild who had Down syndrome. The child had just died.*

> *This professor asked me, 'Paige, how did you accept your*
> *sister's death?' I burst out crying. Then she read my letter*
> *to the entire class. I had forgotten that she even had it.*

Paige knew college was going to be an uphill climb for her. Her second semester average was 1.4 - a D - and her cumulative average was a 1.9, barely a C. But by the next fall semester she managed to bring her overall GPA up to a 2.3, a solid C.

There's more to college than academics, and Paige took full advantage of UMF's extracurricular opportunities. She especially liked the Intervarsity Christian Fellowship. One weekend she attended a Bible and Life Retreat, which made a strong impression on her.

In Paige's words,

> *The Lord really touched me at the retreat and said*
> *that he had something he wanted me to do. I prayed,*
> *saying, 'Lord whatever you want, you're going to have*
> *to show me what it is.'*

> *The next Monday at the university I was sitting*
> *in the Snack Bar when this lady came to my table*
> *where I was eating lunch and said, 'Are you Paige?'*
> *I replied, 'Yes, and who are you?' She said, 'I'm*
> *JoAnne Putnam.' She said she was the chairperson of*
> *the Special Education Department and knew a lot*
> *about Down syndrome. 'I think we can use you, she*
> *said.' I said, 'How?' She said, 'Talking about your*
> *experiences.' I replied, 'No way are you going to ever*

get me to talk in front of other people.'

The Lord quickly let me know that He would give me
the strength I needed to do this. He showed me that
He had given me a talent and that I should use it.

Paige was discovering her gift of speaking about the concerns of people
with disabilities. She wished to contribute to the world, to do God's
will.

When Paige decided that her goal was to work with young children
with special needs, she knew that she would have to further her education. She wanted to do more than change diapers, bathe, and feed
them as she had at Apple Creek and at Sandy River nursing home. She
wanted to transcend custodial care. She wanted to be a teacher.

Another important aspect of teaching children with disabilities besides educating the youngsters, was working effectively with parents of
children with special needs - supporting them, listening to them, and
guiding them to resources. Paige understood that the entire community needed to become more aware and informed about the appropriate educational treatment of persons with disabilities. She wanted to
inculcate the world with the wisdom of not subjecting children to the
devastating effects of segregation and institutionalization.

A chronic problem that affected Paige's ability to learn and interact
with others was her hearing. Nothing had ever been done about her
auditory impairment that was identified when she was first admitted to
Apple Creek at age 15. But the frustration of not being able to hear her
professors and classmates convinced her that it was time to do some-

thing about her disability. It was determined that she had a significant hearing loss, so she submitted an application to Vocational Rehabilitation for financial assistance for a hearing aid. She also requested financial support to defray the costs of college.

In order to process her application, she was told, a representative from vocational rehabilitation would need to inspect her apartment. According to Paige, someone, possibly her mother, had raised fears that Paige was incapable of living independently. She remembers the inspector opening her refrigerator, peering into her closets, and examining the bathroom for cleanliness. The inspector must have been disappointed, because he found a neat and organized apartment.

Nonetheless, the vocational rehabilitation official denied Paige's request for assistance in funding college. The office did provide funds for the purchase of hearing aids. Now in her thirties, Paige finally had a comprehensive hearing evaluation and a prescription for hearing aids. With the hearing aids, she could clearly discern what her professors and fellow students were saying. Auditory learning became less exhausting and less of a struggle, and transformed into further intellectual enlightenment.

Paige's only recourse for tuition assistance was to take out a student loan. She did so, knowing it would take many years to repay. She also kept working nights at the nursing home. In May, 1987, she was awarded her Associate's Degree in Early Childhood Education at the university's graduation ceremony. She reveled in her achievement.

While proud of her accomplishment, Paige sensed that she was not ready to leave the university. She had participated in a number of field placements in early childhood settings. Her greatest joy came from working with young children with disabilities and their families. Although she may not have realized it, she served as a living inspiration to parents of children with Down syndrome and other genetic disorders.

Many early childhood settings in the 80's, however, were not well prepared to serve young children with disabilities. Caregivers indicated that they were inadequately trained to meet the needs of these special children. At the time, my colleagues and I at UMF were awarded a grant to initiate a new program for preparing educational personnel to serve young children with special needs.

We needed to form a steering committee for our grant, and Paige was a natural choice. She was enthusiastic about the new bachelor's degree program and decided that she wanted to be one of the first students to be admitted. Once the pilot program was officially approved by the University of Maine System, Paige applied for admission. Dr. Betsy Squibb, her faculty advisor from the Early Childhood Program, wrote a glowing recommendation for Paige's admission to Wendy Ault, Assistant Director of Admissions.

March 3, 1987

Wendy Ault
Assistant Director of Admissions
University of Maine at Farmington
Farmington, ME 04938

Dear Wendy,

I am very pleased to write a letter of support for Paige Barton's application for admission to the four-year program in Special Education. I have known Paige since spring 1985 as her advisor and instructor in UMF's Associate Program in Early Childhood Education.

From the moment I first met and interviewed Paige, I was tremendously impressed by her. She has a clear and serious commitment to working with young children. She can articulate her goals superbly.

When she entered the two-year program, her intent was to pursue her interest at the two-year level. She was unsure about her success in college work but was determined to do her best. During the past two years I have watched her grow steadily. She works very hard. She takes advantage of the Writing Laboratory and re-writes a paper until she and the instructor are satisfied. In an effort to master a task, she will put in extra time and extra work. She is articulate and takes a leading role in class discussion.

Paige's work with young children is equally impressive. She thoroughly enjoys young children and her enthusiasm is readily apparent. Additionally, she has empathy with individual children. Paige has an in-depth understanding of developmental tasks children are experiencing. She is skilled at observing individuals and planning for their growth.

Paige holds a special place in her professional goals for young children with atypical or special needs. Foremost in her interest are children

with Down syndrome. Based on personal experience, Paige has a tre-
mendous insight to offer young children with Down syndrome and their
families. She is one of those rare individuals who is able to capitalize
on her own trials as one diagnosed as a child with Down syndrome, and
offer support to others.

Paige therefore combines personal and professional goals in her work.
Her personal strengths include perseverance, maturity, and an outgoing
and engaging personality. Paige has few weaknesses. One might be that
Paige occasionally has expectations that are too high. It is these high stan-
dards that have helped her accomplish so much, yet occasionally she needs
to readjust her expectations to be more realistic. For example, Paige may
work extremely hard and receive a "B" in a class. If judged on amount
of energy, work, and learning, she deserves an "A". If judged by quality
of the tasks themselves, her work may be in the "B" or "C" range. Her
difficulty is in reconciling that hard work does not end in all "A's." Paige
is realistic about not pulling all "A's," however, although she would like
to. And, I am sure at some point in her college career, she will attain
this goal. This struggle with her high standards, therefore, can be both a
strength and a weakness.

In sum, I recommend Paige very highly for further work at the col-
lege level in special education. She has excellent potential for contribu-
tion as an educator. If you have any questions, please don't hesitate to
contact me.

Sincerely,

Betsy Squibb, Ph.D.
Associate Professor of Early Childhood Education

Dr. Squibb's evaluation of Paige's capabilities was insightful in raising
the paradox that her high expectations were Paige's greatest weakness
- yet her greatest strength. For these high expectations and standards

accounted for Paige's ultimate victories. She was idealistic in setting worthy goals for her life, and she was optimistic that she would attain them. Her strong will carried her through the gauntlet of her family's pessimism and the lack of confidence of her former teachers and institutional personnel. Except for the willingness of UMF professors and admissions staff, like Dr. Squibb, Dr. Loraine Spenciner, and Wendy Ault and Jim Collins in the admissions department, who went out of their way to support Paige and to accept her challenges and uniqueness, she would not have become a shining advocate for people with disabilities; she would have bloomed unseen.

The admissions committee accepted Paige as a student in the very first class of the Early Childhood Special Education Program. Professor Squibb was accurate in predicting that Paige had excellent potential to become an educator. However, the type of educator Paige would evolve into was unknown to everyone at the time, including Paige.

College life should never be all work and no play, and Paige's days were like those of many coeds: filled with freedom, fun, and the joys of friendship, all of which were nearly impossible to achieve in a residential facility. Although Paige had patient and staff acquaintances in her former institutions, these relationships were not characterized by the spontaneous give-and-take that occurs among true friends. She had encountered very caring staff, but they were hired as helpers - and never really accepted Paige as their equal.

In addition to regular lunches at the university snack bar, group study sessions, and the Christian Intervarsity Club, Paige was an officer in the Special Education student organization. The group was committed to teaching people about exceptionalities and special education. Paige also participated in sign language classes and performances. She loved sign-mime theater, and years later would use her sign language talents to perform with music before thousands of people.

Plainly, Paige's social life was rich, but one thing was missing: a close relationship with a man. It seemed that all the young women she knew at the university had someone to date or to whom they were committed. Fantasies of a man who would love her left Paige longing for male companionship. But she put these unfulfilled dreams aside while she concentrated on her studies and pursued extracurricular activities. Besides, she was still affected by the sexual assault of her job supervisor at the Lake County Mental Retardation Center.

Some of Paige's closest friends were majoring in special education and speech correction. They comprised a fairly tight-knit group of young women who were serious students. They often studied together, sharing their strategies for succeeding in classes, such as techniques for coping with difficult professors, or grappling with challenging or highly technical subject matter. They also had a frivolous side to their interactions and would "party" at the slightest provocation. One good friend, Missy, invited Paige to her home at Thanksgiving, and Paige basked in the warmth and welcome of a traditional New England family gathering.

The simplest things can nurture the human spirit - friendship and family can fill a life with great meaning and deep joy. The fellowship and fun Paige had at the university were some of the most rewarding and meaningful experiences of her life.

The National Down Syndrome Congress

The first evening Paige presented her life story to my special education class induced me to call Diane Crutcher, Executive Director of the National Down Syndrome Congress, to let the organization know about Paige and her remarkable story. Dianne suggested that I submit a presentation proposal for their annual convention. At the time, I was flooded with papers to grade, lectures to prepare, and a research project, not to mention attending to my two young boys, ages 1 1/2 and 5. My archaeologist husband, David, was starting up his field season and taking graduate courses at The University of Maine, in Orono, so he was as busy as I was and could not often fill in as Mr. Mom.

I suggested to Paige that she develop a presentation proposal by the end of January, 1987 and submit it to the conference committee. Paige agreed to write the proposal on the grounds that I would edit it. She really didn't know the magnitude of what she was getting into. In fact, she probably had never attended a national conference before. In hindsight, I'm glad she didn't know what she was getting into because she might not have gone through with it.

Paige had prodigious follow-through. If she promised to do something, it would be done. And, it would be done in a timely fashion. A professor's dream is that all of her or his students would be so conscientious! I suspect that Paige had many late nights studying and completing her assignments. I know she had to study twice as much as most college students. As Dr. Squibb noted, she spent many hours at the Writing Laboratory reworking papers until they were acceptable to her professors. As an example of her diligence and insights, Paige's proposal was a minor masterpiece.

February 17, 1987

Ms. Diane Crutcher
National Down Syndrome Congress
180 Dempster Street
Park Ridge, IL   60068-1146

Dear Ms. Crutcher:

My name is Paige Barton and I would like to be considered as a speaker at the National Convention on Down's Syndrome. I feel I have a story that could bring some hope to parents of children with Down Syndrome and to people with Down's Syndrome.

I have Mosaic Down's Syndrome and have overcome a lot of things. I will be graduating from the University of Maine at Farmington with my Associate Degree in Early Childhood in May. A lot of people said this could not be done but it was something I wanted and have proven that if we put our minds to something we can accomplish it. There are three areas which I would like my speech to bring out:

(a) My experience in an institution and when I got out.

I was put into an institution at the age of 15 and was in different institutions for the next 15 years. I didn't belong in the institution and it was very hard for me to adjust to the situation. I had been in the public schools until this time and was getting C's but my mother had taken me out and put me into the institution. I couldn't understand why my mother had done this. I didn't find out until three years ago that I have Down's Syndrome.

When I finally got out of the institution, I had to learn how to live all over again. It was hard, but somehow I overcame the situation and am now enjoying my freedom. I think one of the main things that helped me is two weeks after I got out I became a Christian. I feel God knew

I would accept Him when I had a chance and He protected me while I was in the institution.

B) Goals I have set and barriers I have faced trying to achieve these goals.

My first goal was set while I was still in the institution and that was to get my G.E.D. This was hard to do as, at that time, there were no educational programs. I got the book and studied on my own with some help from one of the guidance counselors. I took the test in June, 1979 and passed everything.

My second goal was to get out of the institution and become more independent by living on my own. In September, 1980 I got out of the institution and moved to Maine. I worked as a live-in housekeeper for a retired dentist for three years.

My third goal was to get a full-time job and support myself. In September, 1983 I got a job in a Nursing Home in Farmington. I worked as a housekeeper for two years and had my own apartment. I was always told that a person who was handicapped would never be able to do things like living on our own and holding down full-time jobs. A lot of the barriers I've faced are the fact that society tends to believe that people with handicaps are not able to hold down jobs and aren't entitled to things that other people are but we as people know not to underestimate us. We can do anything we put our minds to.

My last goal hasn't been fulfilled yet but I'm working on it. That is to get my degree from college. I love working with children and would like to get my Bachelor's in Special Education for the preschooler. I will get my Associate's in Early Childhood in May and am hoping to get into Special Education in the fall. This was another barrier I faced - the fact that my family and a lot of people said I couldn't accomplish this. It hasn't been easy and it isn't over yet but I feel I can accomplish this goal. It may

*take me longer than some people, but I can do it. I don't know where the
funds are coming from for me to come back as I get no support from my
family but I know God knows how to find ways for things like this if we
put our trust in Him. I think my favorite saying is "I can do all things
through Christ who strengtheneth me." Phillipians 4:13.*

c) How persons with Down's Syndrom can make a difference.

*I feel one way we can make a difference is by setting goals for ourselves
and accomplishing them. I feel by doing this we can let society know that
they should never underestimate what we can accomplish.*

*I am taking a sign language class at this time and if possible would like
to sign a song at the Convention. The song's title is "Touch Through
Me."*

Thank you for considering me to speak.

*Sincerely yours,
Paige Barton*

With a little editing, the proposal went to the conference planning
committee. The following March, Paige received an invitation from
Diane Crutcher to speak.

The following excerpts from Crutcher's letter dated March 13, 1987,
described the audience she would be addressing:

> *Our audience is primarily parental but a good many
> are also professionals somewhere in the Down syn-
> drome arena. Since our primary interest relates to*

> *Down syndrome, we do request that your presenta-*
> *tion center around it. Plenary session attendance is*
> *expected to be 2,000 with the average workshop size*
> *125. The plenary sessions and selected workshops*
> *will be professionally audiotaped. Unfortunately, a*
> *limited budget prohibits payment of an honorarium,*
> *however, in cases of need as designated by the present-*
> *er and the National Down Syndrome Congress, some*
> *travel expenses may be covered.*

When the acceptance letter arrived, I immediately called Paige, asking her to come to my office. She came right over and read the letter. Her first question zeroed in on the magnitude of what she was committing to: "What is a plenary session?" She continued reading the letter aloud. "OH MY WORD!" she shouted. "It says in this letter that the plenary session attendance is expected to be about 2,000!" She looked at me directly, sternly inquiring, "What have you gotten me into?"

Thankfully, the conference planners offered to cover Paige's travel expenses. Just thinking about Paige presenting to 2,000 people made me nervous, and I wasn't even on the program. The largest audience I had ever spoken to was 700! Yet I knew Paige had an important message that needed to be heard - especially by parents. She proved her speaking abilities in my classes, and I was convinced that she could deliver a moving speech. My plan was to accompany her to Washington, DC.

Later that month I found out that I could not go - a trip to China I had applied for had been approved and I would be traveling to Tibet with my husband. Paige would have to go to the conference without me.

I'll never know how she mustered up the courage to take her first airline flight. But she did, and the conference went well. According to many sources, Paige was a grand coup. Her speech encapsulated her past, but the major focus was on setting goals and the importance of an education. Paige never failed to point out the devastating effects of labeling and mislabeling people - and thereby branding them. She ended the session by signing the song she had practiced in her sign-mime class called "Touch Through Me." She made me very proud to be her professor and advisor.

Paige being introduced by JoAnne Putnam for a class presentation at the University of Maine at Presque Isle

Paige signing the song "Tough Through Me" during a presentation

Paige and First Lady Barbara Bush, National Children's Rehabilitation Hospital, June 1990

Paige at the University of Maine at Farmington graduation May 1991

Chapter 8

Designer Genes

It is always the minorities that hold the key of
progress; it is always through those who are unafraid
to be different that advance comes to human society.
-Raymond B. Fosdick

As our friendship flowered, Paige and I tried to unravel her past. The mystery of her disability led both of us to want to understand it better. We wondered whether she truly had Down syndrome, and the longer I knew her, the greater was my distrust of the veracity of her Down syndrome diagnosis. I was beginning to entertain questions about the disparity between her intellectual capabilities and what I believed to be true about most persons with Down syndrome. I confess that my doubts were fueled by my own misguided prior conditioning and low expectations for persons with Down syndrome.

I knew the first step in solving the mystery was to have Paige's blood tested for chromosomal abnormalities. Given her recent notoriety and her future plenary session speech at the national Down Syndrome convention, I wondered whether she would be willing to risk the possibility, however remote, that she might not have Down syndrome. People were taking notice of her and locally she was receiving invitations to speak in other university classes, and in front of public groups. Furthermore, she had lived for 35 years, most of that time under the specter of the Down syndrome or deprecating "mongoloid" label. For the first time, it was working somewhat to her advantage. Why would she want to give it up now? I think the fact that she made an appointment for genetic testing attests to her honorable intentions. Almost like the hero of Oedipus (without his flaw) she was more concerned with finding the truth rather than capitalizing on her recent popularity.   She spoke with her physician, who requested several laboratory tests be conducted at Franklin Memorial Hospital on May 11, 1987.

At the time, Paige had no medical insurance, compelling her to pay for this test herself. I felt terrible about the expense, because the bill turned out to be $340.00! With an income of about $500 a month from Sandy River Nursing home, it was impossible for her to come up with this amount. And with my meager salary of $20,000 and David's and my debt from college loans and the house we had purchased in Farmington, we couldn't cover it, either.

Even more frustrating than the bill was the outcome of the testing, conducted June 1, 1987 by the Eastern Maine Medical Center Cytogenetics Laboratory. A karyotype analysis (study of the chromosomes) of the peripheral blood lymphocytes revealed a diagnosis of 46XX. The report stated that her "Karyotype is consistent with a chromosomally normal female and is also consistent with a previous report dated 12-27-83." In layman's terms, the results were negative. That is, there was no evidence of Down syndrome or any other chromosomal abnormality.

The report just didn't make sense. Equally as upsetting, if not more so, was the realization that the nursing home where Paige had worked had also prescribed a karyotype of Paige's blood to be given as part of a comprehensive physical exam. Paige herself was unaware that the test had been conducted, which certainly to my mind raised some questions about ethics. I wondered, *how would I feel if the university secretly tested my blood for chromosomal abnormalities without telling me?* But the results were the same: negative. If only Paige had known about the karyotype in 1983, she could have saved $340.00 for a test that had already been conducted and yielded the same results.

Dissatisfied with the blood test reports, and still plagued by doubts, I felt that we needed to talk to someone with expertise in genetics. I called the Eastern Maine Medical Center in Bangor to arrange an appointment with a well-known geneticist, Dr. Paul LaMarche.

Over six months later, in January, 1988, we drove for two hours on icy roads for Paige's appointment in Bangor. Dr. LaMarche told us that to obtain an accurate diagnosis, we would probably have to dig deeper, literally. He advised taking a skin sample for analysis, and if nothing turned up then, a bone marrow sample should be drawn. A bone marrow test was the most invasive one, but it would give the clearest picture of the cells. I found Dr. LaMarche to be very approachable. He opened the conversation by telling us that many people have chromosomal abnormalities and aren't even aware of them. Often, he said, medical researchers in the field of genetics will look at their own cells during medical school only to find some atypical cells in their own samples. He had even discovered some abnormalities in his own cellular make-up. His story immediately set Paige at ease.

While Paige had left his office in order to prepare for the skin test, Dr. LaMarche spent some time alone with me. The first thing he did was to admonish me - gently, with a smile, he said: "What ever made you think she has Down syndrome? You ought to know better given the doctoral training you have had in Down syndrome! She has no saddle nose, no 'mongoloid' slant to the eyes, and no high arch in her palate. She does have a short thumb, short little fingernail and little finger with only one joint, a short neck, and a full frontal brow," he asserted. "But the giveaway is the keyhole iris. Can't believe you didn't notice that!"

I was chagrined, and wrote down everything he said.

He knew that further chromosomal testing would be necessary to determine the exact nature of Paige's genetic problem. Also, he felt it would be important to test her pulmonary function.

As a result of the consultation, Paige bravely decided to have the skin test to be followed by the bone marrow test if the skin test were negative. The tissue test results, reported by Head of the Genetics Lab, Dr. Laurent Beauregard, revealed that a small percentage of Paige's cells were abnormal. In about seven percent of Paige's cells, the 18th chromosome was split into three pieces instead of two. The diagnosis was Trisomy 18, mosaic. Mosaic refers to the fact that only a portion of the cells are affected.

At age 36, Paige finally found the explanation for the puzzling "differences" that had shaped her life and others' reactions to her. Unfortunately, all of her life, she had been treated as if she were mentally retarded when, according to Dr. LaMarche, her brain "had not been affected."

"Whatever retardation she may have was the result of her institutionalization, not her brain," emphatically stated Dr. LaMarche. But she did manifest many of the characteristics of Trisomy 18, which typically include heart defects, and problems with the lungs, kidneys, ears, hands and feet, and atypical facial features.

Dr. LaMarche was generally encouraging about the minimal number of cells affected by the trisomy, but he did voice one concern to me in private. "It's going to be very important for Paige to have close medical monitoring all her life because her cells are more likely to become cancerous than cells of people with a normal genetic make-up." It was the first time I had heard that a chromosomal disorder like Paige's could possibly lead to a greater vulnerability to a malignancy. It frightened me, but I kept quiet about it, knowing that Dr. LaMarche had already warned Paige about close follow-up on her condition. Life isn't fair, I thought. Why should Paige have to deal with all of these physical problems? Hasn't she already had her share of life's difficulties?

Nonetheless, Paige possessed an amazing ability to dismiss her myriad of aches, pains, and illnesses. Of those I knew about, her chronic respiratory problems posed the greatest threat. Sometimes her lungs would fill with fluid so that she could hardly breathe, at which point she would rush to the doctor's office or the emergency room to have them suctioned. The winters were especially difficult for her, and she went through courses of antibiotics to fight the various strains of flu viruses and bacterial infections poised to infect her. She had a chronic cough in the winter, exacerbated by the extremely cold Maine winters and the dry heat inside houses and buildings. With impressive discipline, she controlled her borderline diabetes by carefully watching her diet. Periodically she lost her balance, resulting in embarrassing unexpected falls, bruises, and scraped knees. Her diminishing hearing abilities were worsened by ear infections, but the hearing aids she finally acquired while at the university were enormously helpful.

Paige refused to dwell on her pains and illnesses, stoically keeping them to herself. Her ability to sustain a positive attitude not only kept her chronic illnesses at bay, but likely prevented potential medical problems from actualizing. She refused to give in to fears about her diagnosis of Trisomy 18, which would have filled others with dread and a sense of impending doom.

When she first learned about Trisomy 18, she actually felt relieved. "Finally, I know what is wrong with me," said Paige. But along with the relief that came from greater certainty and understanding, the new knowledge provoked negative but understandable emotions of anger and frustration.

"Fifteen years of my life had been taken away because of the wrong label!" she would angrily exclaim. But her optimistic personality always found the bright side of any situation, so she decided to look at her Trisomy 18 as something unique and distinctive. Wittily, she claimed she had designer genes!

Chromosomal disorders like Trisomy 18 are often caused by an alteration in the number of chromosomes, resulting in duplications or deletions of important genetic material. Most often the mechanism which produces most variations in chromosome number is called nondisjunction, because a given pair of parental chromosomes do not "disjoin," or split properly at conception, when the eggs and sperm fuse (meiosis). Normally, reproductive cells contribute 23 chromosomes from each parent, which form pairs in the new organism for a complement of 46 chromosomes. With nondisjunction, one parent contributes an extra chromosome, resulting in 47 chromosomes in a cell rather than the normal 46.

The prognosis for this rare disorder, which occurs in 1 in 5,000 live births is grim - the literature suggests that fewer than 10 percent of affected children will survive past their first birthday. But children are not statistics. There is documentation of persons with Trisomy 18 who survive longer, with at least 11 known instances of children reaching the age of 10. But there are no reports of people with Trisomy 18 who lived into their late 40s besides Paige. She was definitely the oldest on record.

Children with full Trisomy 18 have a multitude of physical problems, such as heart defects, hearing impairments, neurological problems, and slow post-natal growth. Possible malformations are a very small head (microcephaly), short eyelid fissures and epicanthal folds (an overlap of skin in the inner corner of the eye), clenched fists, and clubbed feet. Chronic illnesses are common, including respiratory infections and pneumonias, ear and eye infections, gastro-esophegal disorders, urinary tract infections, and disorders of the kidney and liver.

In the past, the various malformations and anomalies that occurred as a result of Trisomy 18 - or Edward syndrome - were sometimes mistaken for the more common Down syndrome, or Trisomy 21. To the general public, Trisomy 18 usually meant inability to function physically and mentally, if the baby survived at all. Paige's characteristics had been mistaken for those in Down syndrome, or mongolism, in the 50's, long before Trisomy 18 was identified.

The 700 Club and Graduation

The same month that Paige learned about her chromosomal abnormalities, she was invited to speak on the 700 Club of the Christian Broadcasting Network. Wearing a purple dress, she was eloquent in responding to questions posed by host Ben Kinchlow. When Paige talked about being pulled from public school and sent to the Crippled Children's Center, he could hardly believe her sad fate. He was incredulous that she was institutionalized when she was making C's and D's. "My goodness," he exclaimed, "if they put everyone who made C's in a public institution, they'd wipe it [the public schools] out." He asked Paige to recount a horror story from the institution. She described her two days in solitary confinement at Apple Creek Mental Institution as a punishment for playing tag on the deck when running wasn't allowed.

Paige also talked about her religious conversion. "My life as it is right now is a totally different life than it was in those days," she told him. She quoted her favorite Bible verse, Phillipians 4:13 "I can do all things through Christ who strengtheneth me." She followed the verse by saying, "And that's truly what I have to believe. I want God to take my life and touch through me in any way that He can."

At the conclusion of the interview, Kinchlow marveled at Paige's character, her strength, and her charity.

> *Ladies and Gentlemen, how more eloquently can it*
> *be said? Can it be said more eloquently than that?*
> *Lord, take my life, and use it anyway that you can,*
> *dear Lord. You know, it would be so easy for Paige*
> *Barton to be bitter, angry, hostile - to be unforgiving*

for the people who took 15 years out of her life be-
cause of somebody's mistake! But there's no bitterness,
there's no anger, there's no frustration. WHY? The
answer's simple. Jesus Christ makes the difference.
Because Jesus Christ has made a difference in her life,
Paige Barton is making a difference in the lives of
people across America.

With the Down Syndrome Congress and the 700 Club presentations, Paige's speaking abilities were becoming celebrated, and she was
sought after to share her story. She truly enjoyed the attention and was
convinced that it was her purpose to make a difference in the lives of
people with disabilities.

By her fifth year of her university studies, Paige realized that she would
have to detour from the direct route of obtaining her degree in Early
Childhood Special Education. Although it was very unlike her to give
up on a goal, her grade point average fell short of the 2.50 needed
for student teaching. Raising a grade point average based on nearly a
hundred credits is extremely difficult because each course is only worth
3 credits. Even earning a couple of A's wouldn't lift her average enough
to gain admission to student teaching. Her only hope was to retake
a number of courses. Not only were the courses expensive, she also
would be risking her money should she do poorly. One of the classes
she needed to repeat was General Psychology 101, and she was not
confident that she would do much better after three tries.

Her "temperament and disposition toward teaching" were also problems in her success in proving that she could be a public school teacher.
Although Paige loved children and worked well under the direction of a

teacher, she had difficulty assuming the lead. Some of the inappropriate behaviors that were vestiges of her institutionalization were occur-
ring with greater frequency, such as thumb sucking. It is hard to imagine that she would be able to assume a professional position as a teacher
while still sucking her thumb. The lifelong learning and socialization
problems caused by depraved institutional environments are extremely
difficult to overcome.

Paige had put all her energy and finances toward achieving this specific
goal, but she hit a roadblock in not reaching the academic standards
and dispositions to become a teacher. If she wanted to graduate in
May of 1991, her only recourse would be to change her major to
Liberal Studies, a general education degree requiring only a 2.0 grade
point for graduation.

Relinquishing her dream of a degree in Early Childhood Special Education was a profound setback. Paige was rarely dissuaded from giving up
on an important goal, and she had given the degree all her energy, but
her all was not enough. By anyone else's standards, what Paige had accomplished academically was remarkable, considering her background
and lack of education. Dr. Squibb's cautions were prophetic: in this
case Paige had set her expectations too high.

In life's journey, the closing of one door is often followed by the opening of another. Paige's supportive advisor in Early Childhood Special
Education, Dr. Loraine Spenciner had the difficult responsibility of
counseling Paige out of the special education major. Public school
teaching was not a possibility without student teaching, but she observed that Paige's studies could take another course. With a change
in major to liberal studies, Paige was only one semester away from a

degree, the ultimate route Paige elected to follow.

Graduation was nearing, and she was too excited about obtaining a university degree to fret about having to renounce her desire for a teaching degree. In the fall of 1989, David and I and our two boys moved to Missoula, Montana. I was offered a position at the University of Montana Graduate School of Education. We settled in a beautiful mountainside home near Lolo, and I busied myself with teaching, consulting, and writing. Paige and I kept in touch through phone calls, and I knew how meaningful her graduation was to her. She had aspirations to be the Senior Class Speaker, sending me the following letter, which contained an early draft of a speech she had written. Ultimately she delivered a version of the speech at the Senior Class Banquet.

Senior Class Speaker

> *As a senior about to graduate from the University of Maine at Farmington, I tried out along with eight other seniors to be class speaker at my graduation. I am not sure why being class speaker meant as much to me as it did, but for some reason, I wanted this honor. Maybe it had something to do with the fact that I have worked hard for this diploma and wanted to thank the university for giving me a chance.*
>
> *I knew the competition was going to be tough, but I felt I could handle it. After all, I had more experience public speaking than anyone else. I had my speech all prepared and had rehearsed it several times. I felt confident when*

I went in to give it. Since I knew some members of the selection committee, I felt at ease when giving my speech.

The process of selection was simple. We had to prepare a three-minute speech. There were nine students on the selection committee whom we had to speak in front of.

In the speech we had to say why we wanted to be class speaker and what we would talk about in our speech. I said I wanted to be class speaker because I felt I could represent nontraditional students. My speech would be about having goals, and dreams, and achieving these goals and dreams.

When I started college here at UMF in 1984, I never thought I would be able to come as far as I have. I was not sure I could even get through the Early Childhood Associate Program. I am thankful to the people who not only believed in me but helped me believe in myself. I feel that because of these people and the Lord I have been able to achieve as much as I have here at UMF.

I give Jim Collins in the Admissions Office credit for giving me a chance, when other colleges would not even let me try.

The faculty here have been most helpful and understanding. When I have needed extra help they have been more than willing to help me. The PBS (Program of Basic Studies) Program is one of the greatest things a person could ask for.

I will never forget when I was taking Physical Education for the Young Child. I had never had the experience of "galloping." The instructor decided that I could learn how to gallop and I did. I was then chosen to teach the four and five year olds we were working with how to gallop. I taught the lesson, but in the middle of it my knees gave out and I fell flat on my face on the floor! I was embarrassed, but those kids knew how to gallop when we were done with the lesson. It was because the instructor believed in me that I learned how to gallop and was able to teach the lesson.

After we gave our three-minute speeches came the wait. The committee told us it would be at least a week before we would find out. Only four speakers would be chosen: two for the banquet on Friday night and two for the graduation on Saturday.

I wondered if I had made it or not. I had not heard any of the other people who tried out. I had done my best and just trusted the Lord that His will would be done.

When I went to work three nights later one of the committee members was there. She told me the letters had been sent out and I should get mine on Friday. She said I had a unique situation and that the committee had really enjoyed my speech. I thought that my unique situation was that I had been chosen to represent the nontraditional students and got excited.

I couldn't sleep that night and was at the Post Office first thing in the morning. However, my unique situation ended up being something different than I thought it was.

When I went to the Post Office my letter was there. I wanted to open it but something inside of me said to wait. I went to the Snack Bar and found a couple of friends there. They helped me get enough courage to open the letter. I had been selected as the alternate speaker. What this meant was that I had placed number five in the selection process. The committee wanted me to write a speech that I might not give. If for some reason one of the four speakers could not speak, I would be one of the speakers at the Friday night banquet.

I felt like crap after reading my letter. After thinking I had been chosen after Thursday night, the disappointment was even harder to handle. If the committee had liked my speech so well, then why was I the alternate? It was like so many other times in my life when I have felt rejected. It just did not seem fair.

About ten days before graduation one of the speakers from the banquet on Friday night came to see me. He said he thought my speech was great and he felt I should give it. He was going to introduce me when he was done with his speech and no one else would know. I felt like the Lord had answered my prayer. I was ready and knew everything would work out.

Two days before the banquet I got a call from the Senior
Class President. She had found out what was going to
happen and said I wouldn't be allowed to speak. The
next two days were awful. I felt like a ping-pong ball
being bounced back and forth. I was speaking and then I
wasn't, and then I might be.

In the end everything worked out and I did speak but
when I went to the banquet I didn't know whether I
would be or not. I got many compliments on my speech.
I truly thank the Lord for the way that he is in control of
our lives and in every situation.

Graduation day, May 18, 1991, was a triumph for Paige. In the audience were family and friends. Ms. Barton and Paige's brothers and their wives were there, and her friend Missy had driven up from southern Maine. A friend from the Support Organization for Trisomy 18/13 and Related Disorders (SOFT) had driven all the way from Sturbridge, Massachusetts to be there. Paige was touched by their presence, and finally proved to herself and her family that she could succeed in attaining her lofty goals.

She marched up the steps and on to the stage to receive her diploma from the President. The applause and cheers were thunderous. The following are excerpts from the *Franklin Journal*, dated Friday, May 17, 1991 (p. 1):

A Farmington woman who spent [15] years of her
life in an institution because of an incorrect medical
diagnosis, has put part of her life behind her and will

> *be tossing her cap into the air with the University of*
> *Maine at Farmington's other graduates Saturday.*
>
> *Thirty-nine year old Paige Barton finished her last*
> *exam Wednesday morning. And after six and a half*
> *years of study at the university, she's ready to don her*
> *cap and gown and pick up her Bachelor of Science*
> *Degree in General Studies with a 2.47 average.*

"I just finished my last take home and I was jumping," she said laughing with excitement. "I said, Yes, I am out of here."

Paige had a great appreciation for the University of Maine at Farmington and the willingness of faculty to give her a chance, and to teach her well.

> *It [Farmington] was the only school that would even*
> *look at me. I applied to others but they wouldn't*
> *touch me with a 10-foot pole. They believed I could*
> *do it and they helped me believe it.*
>
> *UMF is the school that helps people believe in them-*
> *selves and shoot to do the best that they can. And*
> *they have the support systems to help you do the best*
> *you can.*

Paige's achievements and her devotion to the faculty, staff, and students of the University of Maine at Farmington represent a great tribute to this university. Teachers and schools leave a lasting imprint on their graduates. In Paige's situation, she was earning more than a degree; she was earning her dignity and self-respect. The time had come for her to make a return on her alma mater's investment in her. She was determined not to "rest on the laurels" of her new diploma for very long.

Chapter 9

SOFT Touches

Do not mistake a child for his symptom.
-Eric Erickson

Reflecting on her life on graduation day, Paige certainly had a right to revel in her many accomplishments. Since her release from the Lake County Mental Retardation Center, she had earned her high school general equivalency degree, landed a full - time job, and achieved a university degree. It was now time to put her education and experience to work. The future looked very bright, and she had a dream to fulfill.

In 1988, shortly after Paige discovered that she had Trisomy 18 - mosaic, she heard about an organization called Support Organization for Trisomy 18, 13 and Related Disorders (SOFT). SOFT President, Pat Farmer, an Idaho Regional Special Education Consultant and Special Education Instructor at Idaho State University, contacted Paige after she heard about her at a conference for families whose children had Down Syndrome. She mentioned to one of the presenters that she had a son with Trisomy 13, and the presenter gave her my name and phone number at the University of Maine at Farmington. Pat wrote about her first contact with Paige in the *SOFT Times* newsletter:

> *'What will I say to her?' I asked my husband on that*
> *day in June 1988. 'People with Trisomy 18 are not*

supposed to be able to talk,' I said. I was so nervous.
I paced back and forth. 'What will I say?'

Days before I had attended a conference with a friend
for families whose children had Down syndrome.
As I visited with one of the presenters and told her
about my son with Trisomy 13, she said, 'I know
someone you need to talk to.' She told me about a
woman with Trisomy 18 who lived in Maine and
was going to college. She said she was in her thirties.
I was stunned! I couldn't believe it. She gave me the
name of one of her college professors and said to call
and visit with her. I did and she encouraged me to
call this woman named Paige Barton. She said she
would tell her I would be calling.

I finally had the courage to call this woman named
Paige Barton. She said she would tell her I would be
calling. I finally had the courage to call.

'Hello - is this Paige Barton?' I said. 'Yes it is,' the
woman said. I was shaking. 'I am the President of
a support group for families whose children have
Trisomy 13 or 18,' I said. 'I have Trisomy 18,' she
replied. 'Really?' I said back. Then we laughed
and the friendship began. It was a moment I will
never forget. We immediately began to make plans
to get her to the Philadelphia conference . . . only
a few short weeks away. (SOFT Times, November/
December 1999, p.9)

Although SOFT had managed to arrange for funding to partially finance Paige's expenses, she still needed to come up with $500.00 for the airline ticket. I was optimistic that someone would support Paige's cause, so I told her not to worry about it, that somehow we'd find the money. Off the top of my head, I suggested that she ask the UMF Provost if he might have some suggestions for paying for her trip. While Paige was in his office, he phoned the financial aid office. Shortly, the Director of Financial Aid called me to verify Paige's conference plans, and, presto, she had her travel money - all $500.00.

Several SOFT members, Steve Cantrell and John Harper, had agreed to meet Paige at the airport and drive her to the conference hotel. Steve and Peggy Cantrell remembered being surprised by their first encounter with Paige:

> *John Harper asked me to go with him to the airport to pick up Paige. We arrived at the gate and the plane was late. John and I both wondered if Paige would be mobile or would need assistance to get around. Well, all the passengers finally were off the plane, and no one who we thought even slightly resembled anyone with special needs had gotten off the plane. Then out of the corner of our eye there was Paige, smiling, no not just smiling, beaming ... and we knew that was Paige. The ride back was full of excitement because Paige had begun to meet her extended family and we had begun to meet her! Paige connected with everyone and somehow made all of us feel better about being there and to somehow look beyond our physical challenges. (SOFT Times, November/December 1999, p. 10)*

A videotape produced at the Philadelphia conference shows Pat Farmer introducing Paige at the opening session. Dressed in an eye-catching bold black and white striped dress, Paige stood behind a massive wooden podium in a large ballroom. The audience was hushed with the exception of the coos and cries of the children, mostly in strollers and wheelchairs, attending the conference with their parents. Her composure was amazing, especially considering her inexperience in public speaking. The first words she uttered to this very special group of families were filled with enthusiasm and gratitude. It was as if she had found her long lost family.

"This convention is incredible!" she told the audience. "I came here expecting something, but what I expected wasn't anything like this. This is beyond anything that I could have imagined . . . I didn't know that this group existed, and when Pat called, I wondered how I would get here . . . and miracles never cease to amaze me."

Paige went on to explain how the university provided the money for her to fly to Philadelphia. Her voice started to quaver as she said, "I just want to thank God that someone came up with that money for me to be here. These kids out here are beautiful children, and you are all beautiful people. I just want to say that this convention is called SOFT Touches, and this afternoon you're going to hear something that is my theme, which is Touch Through Me. A lot of you people here had children that have died and I think it's incredible that anyone who has lost a child still supports a group like this." The audience broke into a loud applause. Later during the conference she made a presentation, signing the song Touch Through Me. Promptly she was invited to be an honorary member of the Board of Directors.

Karen Dewy wrote about the Philadelphia conference and the impression she had of Paige and her profound impact on the SOFT families and organization:

> *As I step into the hotel, in awe and wonder that we were really here, my ears pick up on something. It's true. There really is a woman that has Trisomy 18 and can walk, talk, and is actually going to go to college, and she's here! Thus I was first introduced to Paige Barton.*
>
> *She was a little different from what I had expected. No shy one, Paige became the darling of the conference. New hope that our children could survive, and not only that, for some of the mosaic children, a wonderful, normal future. Paige held our son, Mark, and cried along with us. What compassion she had for the kids... There are coincidences, but was our knowing Paige one of those? I think not. Paige was sent to us in Philadelphia for a reason. Her presence became a catalyst for SOFT. Through time, many families have seen Paige, and our other elders, and fought for their own children. (SOFT Times, November/December 1999, p. 8)*

Paige was bursting with excitement when she returned to Farmington after the conference. She even had a gift for me from the conference - a red softball cap with the letters SOFT printed in white above the bill. Although I am not exactly the cap type, I proudly placed it on my head and hugged her in appreciation. She was always so thoughtful, and I had no choice but to loosen up and put on the cap. We both laughed at how out-of-character I appeared in the cap.

When I asked her how the sessions and presentations went at the conference, she told me she had learned much new information about her disorder and she heard explanations for her kidney, hearing, and respiratory problems. Out of the former chaos, her medical problems were starting to make sense!

She had met Dr. John Cary, a physician and professor at the Department of Pediatrics/Medical Genetics at the University of Utah. Although he was a well-known international expert in pediatric genetics, he was also a very approachable and caring man. As the SOFT Medical Advisor, he was held in high esteem by the parents, and Paige agreed whole-heartedly. Dr. Cary obviously cared more about Paige the person than Paige the case study, the oldest known living person with Trisomy 18 - mosaic.

"The mosaic form of Trisomy 18 - mosaic is nothing like full blown Trisomy 18," he explained. Nor did he find it surprising that Paige wasn't made aware of her chromosomal problem for most of her life. Dr. J.H. Edward first described the syndrome in 1960 in the British Journal, *Lancet*. By the mid sixties genetic testing was available to most hospitals; however, skin biopsies were rarely conducted, and infants and young children were more likely to be tested than teens and adults. Typically, diagnoses were arrived at by describing the individual's morphological characteristics (a person's structure and form). To obfuscate matters, genetic testing was not - and generally still is not - covered by insurance, as MRI's or CAT scans are.

Dr. Cary believed that diagnoses are made to predict the pattern and problems of a syndrome in order to promote an individual's well-being. For example, he told Paige she would need to continually monitor her kidney function. He also suggested that she see a neurologist at Mt. Sinai Hospital in New York to better understand her physical problems.

Dr. Cary never examined Paige. He refused to "medicalize" her, insisting that she was not a statistic.

"Paige was unquantifiable," he said. "Her legacy," he told me, "is what she gave to SOFT parents - hope. Hope is not about statistics, hope is not about living to your 40's. That's irrelevant. She rose above 'nature and nurture' to achieve her dreams. Her appearance was different and she capitalized on it to teach others. She used the power of her personality, which was magical."

I asked him if parents would be disheartened to meet Paige knowing that, unlike Paige, most children with Trisomy 18 die in infancy. "Does it give parents false hope?" I asked. "False hope is an oxymoron!" he replied. "The real tragedy is when people place false ceilings on children." Paige had broken through the ceiling of longevity statistics, the dire medical prognoses of her genetic disorder, and her disadvantaged childhood.

> *Doctors tend to treat the rule, not the exception.*
> *With help, we may be able to change that by draw-*
> *ing on information and experience. (Trisomy 18: A*
> *Handbook for Families, 1999)*

In addition to the many wonderful people she met at the Philadelphia SOFT conference, Paige's participation in her first SOFT balloon launch was one of the most memorable events of the trip.

Many of the parents attending the SOFT conference had lost their children to Trisomy 18 or 13 - some very recently - and were still grieving. To commemorate their beloved children, the conference held a balloon launch. Parents, family members, and friends were given colorful helium balloons to release in honor of a child or loved one who had passed away. The child's name, birthdate, and the date the child passed away were written on the balloon. Paige emotionally described the scene of dozens of balloons floating into the sky. Tears rolled down her cheeks as she released a balloon for her sister Heidi, who had died in her 20s of diabetes.

I think the balloon launch caused her to pause and mull over her own mortality. "I realized that I am a walking talking miracle because I am the oldest known person with Trisomy 18. In my darker moments, I feel that Trisomy 18 is a death sentence," admitted Paige. "I have no idea how long I will live . . . then again, who does?"

At the conference, Paige made some great contacts with parents of children with Trisomy 18 and 13, who lived up to their promise to call and keep in touch. One couple, Steve and Peggy Cantrell, even invited her to their home in St. Louis for Christmas. Again, the plucky Paige didn't hesitate to accept!

"I'm going to call and send cards to these families," she pledged. "If there is a mother and a father with a new baby who has Trisomy 18 or 13, I will talk to them," Paige said. "And, I'm going to try to go to every SOFT conference from now on! Period!" As the Cantrells observed,

"Paige had finally found a family that accepted her unconditionally for just herself."

Paige took her promises seriously, and she fulfilled most of them. For 12 consecutive years, she called Pat Farmer on her son Joey's birthday. And, she was forced to miss only a few SOFT conferences.

Paige's life revolved around being able to help others. "Why was it so difficult for nondisabled people to understand that people with disabilities don't always want to be on the receiving end of a relationship?" she wondered. She sincerely wanted to console the SOFT families who were coping with the difficulties of parenting a child with a severe disability. As Dr. Cary pointed out, she was able to instill hope in parents because she herself had lived so long and purposefully, and thus was an example. Conversely, it made her feel worthwhile to be able to give something back to these wonderful families who cared so much about her.

Barb Van Herreweghe, President of SOFT at this writing, remembers her first encounter with Paige in Philadelphia. "How could it be possible that there was someone alive over 30 years old with any form of T-18? Well, you bet we wanted to hear the whole story. That we did. There were not too many dry eyes in the house when she spoke."

Barb wondered about parallels between her child and Paige.

> *Could our child possibly be like Paige? Probably not, but she gave us the hope to continue to move on in our lives and keep fighting for our children. Although she was as scared as all of us, she spoke with confi-*

dence and ease! She didn't know any of us, either. She visited with us over the weekend, joined us for dinner, and just gave of herself as she has done for years after that first meeting.

Kris Holladay, who founded SOFT with her husband Hal, reminisced that when she first learned about Paige, she literally fell off her chair.

I remember the phone call from Pat Farmer like it was yesterday! On the phone Pat asked me if I was sitting down. I replied that I was and Pat said, 'Good, you're gonna' need to be sitting down for this one!' Pat then went on to tell me about a conversation she just had on the phone with a dynamic and delightful woman named Paige Barton. Nice, I thought, but not enough to make the earth - or the chair - move. Pat's next sentence did indeed cause me to fall off my chair. 'Paige,' she says, 'has Trisomy 18!' I picked myself up, got back into my chair, and started stammering 'She talks on the phone? She goes to college? She lives in an apartment? Are you sure she has Trisomy 18?' Pat went on to explain Paige's incredible story to me.

I could write pages about Paige! We came to know Paige through SOFT. Also, she came to stay with us in Arizona for two months. While visiting in Arizona, she shared her story five times to various organizations - college classes, church groups and a geneticist.

The Holladays were extremely gracious in providing housing for Paige when she moved to Arizona. The position she expected to assume after graduation, however, turned out to be a debacle.

Community Partners

Shortly after graduation, Paige left for Phoenix, Arizona, where she had a job possibility in a child care facility. A letter she wrote to me dated August 28, 1991, was quite brief:

> *On May 25th I moved to Arizona thinking that I had a job with the state. When I got there, I found out the woman who had hired me had resigned. They kept telling me I would be able to go to work by June 15th instead of the 1st. I waited and kept hoping but nothing was happening. On June 15th they said it would be three to six months. I started trying for jobs in the paper but had no luck.*

> *On June 27th I moved back to Maine. I am living in Kennebunkport about 1/2 mile from my parents. I am working two jobs right now. I work in a pizza shop on Tuesday, Wednesday, and Thursday mornings and am a chambermaid on Friday through Monday at one of the inns here.*

Paige was relieved to be back in Maine. She missed her friends from the university, but she accepted the fact that it was time to move on in her life, as she indicated in her letter to me:

*In a way, I'm glad I'm not going back to school. But
I will miss everyone. I am living about thirty minutes away from Missy, which is great. We see quite a
bit of each other. She had a party a few weeks ago,
and I saw Tim and Crissy, which was lots of fun.*

Another indication of Paige's ability to plan and to dream was her
question about the possibility of a book. She prodded me: "Are you
still interested in doing the book? I'm ready. I'm thinking about just
starting and writing the first chapter, I'm enclosing a couple of things
you might like to see," she wrote.

Paige immediately threw herself into finding work near Kennebunk-
port, landing the two menial jobs mentioned in her letter - one at a
pizza shop and the other as a chambermaid at an inn. While she was
thankful for finding work, wiping tables and taking out garbage, and
cleaning rooms didn't require a college education. These jobs did not
pay enough to cover her living expenses and make her payments on her
college loan. It was beginning to appear that her mother's greatest fear
was coming true - that after investing tens of thousands of dollars and
six years into a college education, she would not be able to find suitable
work because of prejudice against people with disabilities.

Paige possessed enough fortitude not to give up on her dreams, not
after all this work...not yet. She resolved to be patient and have faith
that her prayers would be answered. They were.

A contact she made the previous spring while working as a university
intern with the Maine Department of Mental Health, Mental Retardation, and Substance Abuse was about to pay off. Paige met Dick

Tryon, Founder and Executive Director of Community Partners (then called Community Support Services Incorporated - CSSI), a nonprofit agency that provides a range of services to people with mental retardation. They co-presented at one of the first Bill Twarag Lecture Series. Dick remembered the symposium day very well:

> *As I got up to give my address, Paige encouraged me by saying 'break a leg.' Ironically, my mother fell and broke her leg at almost the same time Paige was joking about it. Paige always felt slightly guilty about what she said.*

> *The next year, I offered Paige the opportunity to live in an apartment with Evelyn Johnson, an elderly disabled woman who, due to failing health, needed live-in support in order to stay in her apartment. Paige jumped at the chance to be working with people. Because of Paige's support, Evelyn was able to stay in her own apartment for many more months. Evelyn's health eventually deteriorated to the point where she needed the full-time medical care offered in a nursing home. Paige was able to remain in the apartment and, for the first time, she was really on her own. We continued to visit and be close to Evelyn until her death many years later.*

It was indeed fortunate that Dick remembered Paige from her university internship because in addition to providing her the live-in opportunity with Evelyn, he offered her a part-time job in Biddeford, consuming about three to five hours a week. It wasn't many hours, but the type of work was certainly more meaningful than ignominiously cleaning out toilets and making beds, though she continued doing so to supplement her income.

Initially, the position with Community Partners involved organizing support groups for people with disabilities who wanted to leave group homes and move into their own apartments. Paige herself came up with the job title of "Self-Advocacy Organizer" and helped to write the job description. Not surprisingly, the qualifications for the job fit Paige to a tee. Because of her personal experience with institutional living and the transition to the community living, she understood firsthand the concerns and frustrations of people in similar situations. According to Dick, "Her job was to help other people with disabilities get their own voice and speak up for themselves."

Paige's role as Self-Advocacy Organizer soon escalated into a Worksite Aide position at Riverworks, a restaurant operated by Community Partners. In May, 1992, her time commitment more than quadrupled to twenty hours a week. In this new capacity, she served on behalf of her clients as a spokesperson concerning funding issues. The free room and board was an added benefit as well as a financial necessity for Paige. Given her meager salary, it would have been impossible for her to pay off her student loans and make ends meet without the costs of housing being defrayed.

After Evelyn Johnson moved out, Paige roomed for three years with a woman named Celia, who had moved to Maine from New York and was grateful to live with Paige.

"I was very happy," said Celia. "Paige was always so sweet and laughing. She'd do everything for everybody. She couldn't do more . . . She was a good, responsible friend you could trust. So sincere."

In the evenings, Paige worked at Community Partners' Riverworks, She also helped out at the community meal program, where about 40 people who were living independently would come for meals and to "hang out." Meals were served at tables, rather than in the less dignified cafeteria style of some charity or soup kitchens. Fittingly, the program was called the Bon Apetit Community Meal Program. Bon Apetit became a non-profit organization with its own board. Paige was a member of the Board until she left Biddeford in 1996.

Paige's finances had always been a struggle, and, like many people (including myself), she had succumbed to the temptation of using credit cards to pay for living expenses when her salary wasn't sufficient to cover all costs. Dick pointed out that as she met consumers around the state, she would allow them to call her collect. Then, she would call them back and pay for the call her self. Her phone bill was mounting and she had a college loan to pay off in addition to the credit cards. Every month she was sinking more deeply into debt. Ultimately, she could afford to pay off only the interest on her credit cards, so the principle continued to loom over her head.

Paige was reluctant to tell anyone about her financial problems because she was afraid it might cost her independence. Not knowing where to turn, she asked her friends at Community Partners what to do. A financial advisor recommended that she file for bankruptcy. He could see no other alternative. He set up a tight budget that she had to follow religiously with oversight from the staff at Community Partners. The student loan would still have to be paid, but she was out from under the credit card debt. It was a difficult lesson - a lesson that many Americans learn the hard way.

But Paige kept the faith and her life and finances started to turn around. In March, 1993, the position at Community Partners was upgraded to full time as a Self-Advocacy Organizer. It was a job that meant much more to Paige than meeting her financial obligations - it gave her an opportunity to use her talents and thereby to develop a sense of self-respect. She expressed her gratitude on the Community Partners booklet that featured her story and displayed her picture on the cover:

> *I'm thankful that Community Partners was willing*
> *to give me a chance to achieve my dream of being*
> *employed full time advocating for myself and others.*
> *I have an office with my own desk, I get a paycheck,*
> *and I carry a briefcase - which lets me know that I'm*
> *a professional. (Community Partners Booklet, Bid-*
> *deford Maine)*

The Community Partner's mission, holistically promoting the autonomy of people with disabilities, aligned beautifully with Paige's philosophy of self-determination coupled with support services that provide opportunities for choice and personal growth. Offering over 200 people a variety of day, vocational, and residential programs, ranging from independent living, supported living apartments, Medicaid waiver homes, and intermediate care facilities, it was the ideal organization for her at that stage in her life.

Fortunately, Dick Tryon realized that Paige had the energy and the potential to move beyond Community Partners. Paige accompanied Dick to most professional meetings in Maine, and as a result became a member of many boards and committees in her own right. She was a member of The University of Maine Center for Community Inclusion's Consumer Advisory Committee, The Statewide Independent Living Council, The American Network of Community Options and Resources (the Maine chapter and later the national chapter). She also became involved in legislative actions to create more independent funding options for consumers and was an outspoken advocate to raise pay rates for staff in programs for supporting people with mental retardation and other developmental disabilities.

Paige also started several self-advocacy groups within Community Partners. At one meeting the consumers told Paige they wanted to have a conference and stay overnight at a hotel just like staff did sometimes. This was the seed for the annual Speaking Up for Us conferences, which became her personal mission to accomplish.

The last page of the Community Support Services brochure displays a quotation for which Paige was well known, "In the word 'disability' is the word 'ability' and that's what we wish to convey. We have abilities just like you."

The idea of emphasizing abilities rather than disabilities was the fruit of a seed planted at a very significant event for Paige in 1990, the Annual Victory Award Ceremony in Washington, D.C.

The Hall of Victory

In 1990, Paige was honored by Governor Mc Kernan of Maine as the recipient of the Maine State Victory Award. She would be Maine's representative at the National 1990 Victory Awards in Washington, D.C. That year, President George Bush signed what some people consider to be the most significant civil rights legislation in the last quarter of the century: the Americans with Disabilities Act (ADA), prohibiting discrimination against people with disabilities in all walks of life. The ADA had the potential of affecting over 46 million Americans with disabilities.

The June 26th ceremony was hosted at the elegant John F. Kennedy Center by actor Elliot Gould, who announced the purpose of the awards - a tribute to those who have personally triumphed over adversity with spirit and determination. In Gould's words, "We honor steadfast effort in coping with frightening problems. We honor people who reveal grace under pressure. We honor people who say 'I can' when a practical assessment would say you can't."

Entertainer Loretta Lynn, in a black sequined gown, sang "Coal Miner's Daughter" - her own story of triumph over adversity. Paige was recognized alongside famous Victory honorees such as actress Patty Duke who talked about her battle with bi-polar disorders; I. King Jordan, Gallaudet University's first deaf President; *Roots* miniseries actor Ben Vereen who overcame drug addiction; and radio announcer and entertainment programmer Brian May, paralyzed and respirator dependent from a reaction to the polio vaccine in 1955. The ceremony showed how misfortune can be a great equalizer among people, be they famous or be they humble - all must live each day using what they have left with spirit and determination.

The band played triumphant music as each national recipient marched forward with a state flag bearer as an escort. Resounding in Paige's ears was the announcement: "From the state of Maine . . . PAIGE BAR-TON." That day at the National Rehabilitation Hospital, she met First Lady Barbara Bush. Her picture was taken with the First Lady, a photo she would forever cherish.

I thank you, Governor McKernan and those Mainers responsible for this prestigious nomination. It infused her with pride and suffused her with purpose to "use the hand she was dealt with" in continued service to others.

Speaking Up for Us

One of the first consumers that sought Paige's help when she was employed by Community Partners was a woman named Marcia Rosen. Dick Tryon recounted Marcia's story:

> *Marcia had lived at the Pineland Institution for years, and then moved to a 6-person Intermediate Care Facility operated by Community Partners. Marcia was inspired by Paige and asked for her help in moving into a smaller 3-4 person home. Marcia's family was initially against the move, but after hearing Marcia speak out so well for herself with Paige's support, they agreed. Several years later, Marcia decided she wanted to move into her own apartment.*

Once again, with Paige's support, Marcia initiated the process to move again. Unfortunately, before this move could take place, Marcia died.

It was Paige's first experience with the death of a person she had advocated for and had become very close to.

In memory of Marcia, Paige initiated the "Marcia Rosen Speaking for Ourselves Conference" in 1993. The Rosen family was present for the first award presentation and has donated money to the award each year since.

Paige considered her role in creating the first statewide self-advocacy organization to be her most significant professional accomplishment. In November 1993, under the auspices of Community Partners, she organized the first statewide conference for people with developmental disabilities in Maine. Orchestrating a large conference is an immense task, and no one was sure that she could pull it off, least of all Paige. She had many responsibilities, which included scheduling national speakers and workshop presenters for the two-day conference, reserving rooms for hundreds of participants in accessible hotels, and making transportation arrangements for the participants to travel to and from the conference. Over 300 people attended the first annual conference in '93 and about 400 attended in '94. By 1995, the attendance reached 450 people.

Convening groups this large posed enormous logistical problems, such as finding accessible accommodations for many people using wheelchairs. But Paige was inspired by the tremendous potential of a collective group of individuals with disabilities advocating for themselves. Her experience with SOFT and the Down Syndrome Congress provided some background in what the endeavor would require.

Paige felt strongly about encouraging "consumers" of disability services to speak to legislators and citizens about issues that most affect them. "It is really neat to be able to help a person testify before the legislature for the first time and watch the reaction they get. It gives the person a sense of knowing that they can make a difference. Their voices are being heard and people are listening," said Paige.

Dick Tryon tells of Paige's ability to capture and sustain the attention of lawmakers in the noisy and distracting legislative hearings. "Her ability to command everyone's attention in the room is amazing. Her extemporaneous presentations combined humor, intelligence, humility, and spirituality that captivated everyone in the audience," said Tryon. "She had a tremendous presence in public hearings and had become one of the most effective advocates for people with disabilities in the state."

Paige's direct work with consumers was as important as her active espousal and public relations work - especially to the individual consumers. One woman, who for many years resided in public institutions and group homes, desperately wanted to live on her own. However, her family was opposed to the move because she had epilepsy. Her family was concerned that she would have a seizure when she was alone and no help would be available. It is possible for someone with a seizure disorder to die if unattended during a "status seizure," which may require medical intervention to assist the individual in regaining consciousness.

While the likelihood of a status seizure was remote, it was still within the realm of possibility. But the woman was doggedly determined to move out of the group home - which she detested - and into an apartment. Through Paige's support and advocacy, this woman was able to receive "supported independent living" from Community Partners.

Initially, an aide assisted her for 40 hours per week. Eventually the assistance was reduced to only five or ten hours a week. Paige acknowledged that there were risks involved in living on one's own, but the quality of life that accompanied that risk usually made it worth the hazards.

The notion of "Dignity of Risk" often cropped up in Paige's conversations. To her, dignity of risk entailed having choices and options, and sometimes required taking chances. It meant having the opportunity to succeed as well as the opportunity to fail. Sometimes people pursue new avenues in their lives that do not lead to success, but they may learn more in the pursuit than if they stayed with the tried and true. Such lessons often prepare the way for mastering a new challenge. Paige wrote in the Community Partners Booklet:

> *Let me tell you that even with all the hassles of life,*
> *it's a lot better to be free. God didn't mean for us to*
> *be in a cage, but to fly freely, and reach the greatest*
> *heights we can.*

Like a watch dog, Paige carefully guarded her freedom and the freedom of consumers of disability services to live in the community. Her beliefs also applied to our elders. Nursing homes can strip away freedom just as segregated institutions do - sometimes even more so.

Father's Death

The greatest loss Paige encountered in her life, next to Heidi's death, was her father's passing in 1994. Mr. Barton had been gravely ill and had been hospitalized. When his death appeared imminent, the family was called together. Paige was able to get to Philadelphia to visit with him in the hospital during his final days, a chance for which she was grateful. After the hospital visit, she made a point to tell her family how important it was for her to see him again before he died. She needed to say good-bye. Leaving the hospital, she implored her mother and sisters to be sure to call her during his final hours. But she was never able to say good bye.

Paige mourned her inability to deliver this final farewell to her father, citing it as one more example of her treatment as a non-person, someone who always had to be protected from harsh realities, someone whose voice did not count in family decisions. Paige remembers being told that if she attended the funeral, she must stay in control of her emotions and act like an adult. "Not one tear," she was admonished, as if her grief would humiliate her stoic family.

Dick Tryon speculated that Paige's experience with her father's death motivated her to advocate even more strongly for people with mental retardation to be included in all elements of family grief and loss experiences. Paige initiated the Community Partner's Flower Committee, which still meets to support consumers in grief and loss experiences. The committee also sends cards and flowers to staff and consumers undergoing significant loss.

Pineland Closes

In 1996, a benchmark in the education and treatment of persons with mental retardation invigorated advocates. Pineland Center, Maine's state institution for persons with mental retardation in Pownal, was officially closed. Pineland was Maine's counterpart to Apple Creek, a large state hospital for persons with mental retardation located in a picturesque rural area of Maine about 15 miles north of Portland. Large brick buildings dotted the campus, which was also filled with mature trees and green lawns. Unlike Apple Creek, however, the deinstitutionalization process occurred years earlier because of a court ordered consent decree stipulating that the residents be moved into community settings. By the time of its closure, there were less than one hundred residents: those with more severe disabling conditions and medical needs.

Several years earlier, while attending a meeting at Pineland with her boss, Dick Tryon, Paige encountered someone from her past. The meeting seemed beyond coincidence. She met the new Superintendent, who turned out to be a former staff member from the Lake County Mental Retardation Center in Ohio. Years earlier, she had probably annoyed this man with her youthful antics and misbehaviors. Paige claimed that he once told her she was mentally retarded and that she "wouldn't amount to a hill of beans." "Can you believe this same man was now in Maine - the Superintendent at Pineland?" she told me. "And I sat next to him at a meeting!" According to Dick, "She giggled all the way home from the meeting."

The Pineland Consent Decree was nearly fulfilled, and the institution was to be officially closed. A ceremony was held on the grounds of the institution.

"He had to eat his words," chortled Paige. "He once told me I wasn't worth anything, and he later had to reconcile that insult with the fact that I was sitting next to him, celebrating the closing of the institution - his institution - as a professional woman."

SOFT member and journalist Bob Irvin wrote about the superintendent's unfortunate statement - you are mentally retarded and you won't
amount to a hill of beans - in the *SOFT Times (1999)*:

> *Many times, Paige delivered her statement in her*
> *public presentations. Paige relished turning her old*
> *adversary's statement on its ears. Most people who*
> *knew her believe it may have been the closest she ever*
> *came to a good old-fashioned throwing-someone's-*
> *statement-back-in-their face. Paige was famous for*
> *saying no one was to blame for the lost years of her*
> *life, that the circumstances simply happened the way*
> *they happened for a higher purpose, and that she*
> *would take advantage of them, not succumb to them.*

> *Paige once told her Community Partners Supervisor*
> *Dick Tryon that her Vocational Rehabilitation coun-*
> *selor claimed that she was never going be more than*
> *a chambermaid and therefore a college education was*
> *superfluous. Years later, after obtaining her degree*
> *and while working for Community Partners, she was*
> *invited by this same man to present a workshop for*
> *his staff. He was now the regional manager for the*
> *Department of Mental Health and Mental Retarda-*
> *tion in Portland.*

> *Ah, life has its sweet ironies!*

June 1st, the Pineland closing ceremony took place on the campus
grounds. Keys to the front door were distributed to the attendees as a

keepsake to symbolize the last locking of the door. Paige was asked if she wanted to collect the keys, and she refused: "No, I don't ever want to see one of those keys to the institution again!" She and Vanessa, a friend who once attended Pineland, gathered as many keys as they could find and threw them in the trash can.

Paige with Dixie Leavitt at the Support Organization for Trisomy 18, 13 and Related Disorders (SOFT) conference 1999 in Rochester NY

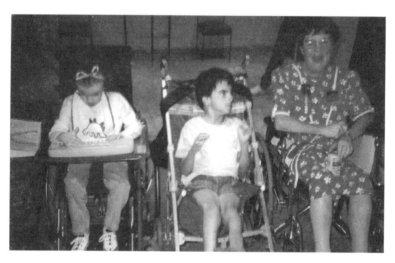

Paige with SOFT friends Kyle Harper and Megan Barnes, early 1990's

Paige and close friend Pat Farmer at a SOFT balloon release Philadelphia 1989

Paige as a Consumer Advocate, supporting people in community living

Paige in a Maine legislative hearing, looking at mentor and friend Richard Tryon of Community Partners

Paige and Steve Cantrell

Paige talking politics with Congressman John Baldacci, now Maine's governor

DEPARTMENT OF MENTAL HEALTH,
MENTAL RETARDATION AND
SUBSTANCE ABUSE SERVICES

PAIGE BARTON
MR/DD PROGRAM COORDINATOR
OFFICE OF CONSUMER AFFAIRS

TEL (207) 287-____
TOLL FREE (800) 588-____
40 STATE HOUSE STATION   FAX (207) 287-____
AUGUSTA, MAINE 04333   TTY (207) 287-____
e-mail: Paige.Barton@state.me.us

Paige's business card

Chapter 10

Consumer Advocate

You can do it. You can speak up for yourself!
-Paige Barton

In the late spring of '96, an exciting possibility emerged for Paige. The Maine Department of Mental Health, Mental Retardation, and Substance Abuse Services (DMHMRSAS - phew!), had received an allocation from the legislature, which Tryon and Paige worked and advocated for, to fund several consumer advocate positions, including a consumer advocate position for people with developmental disabilities. It would be the nation's first cross-disability consumer advocacy office. The position was to be full-time, with a substantial salary of over $20,000.00 (almost double what Paige had been earning), and good medical benefits as she had with Community Partners. With Paige's various health problems, living without medical insurance would be tempting Providence.

Paige applied for the job, lobbied hard, and anxiously waited for several months to hear if she would be selected. There was another qualified applicant for the job, but she knew that the search would be conducted equitably. After what seemed like an eternity, her prayers were answered when she was notified that she had been selected for the position.

Leaving Biddeford and her friends at Community Partners ended up being more difficult than she thought it would be. The last thing she needed was trouble with moving her belongings to Augusta, but trouble found her. Paige's new supervisor was Cathy Bustin Baker, Director of the Office of Consumer Affairs. Cathy and Paige told the story of the moving day fiasco.

> *When I moved from Biddeford to Augusta, the moving company made a mistake on the bill. They were going to charge me for a move from Biddeford to Augusta, Georgia, rather than Augusta, Maine. In order for the State of Maine to reimburse the moving company, the destination on the bill should have been 'Augusta, Maine.' The movers called the owner of the company to straighten things out. I guess he was suspicious about whether the State of Maine was really funding the move, so he asked the Augusta police to make a visit to my new apartment. They needed to verify that my boss really worked for the State and could authorize the billing.*

Cathy, who donned her advocacy hat, remembers that she was ready to play hard ball with the misinformed movers. "There Paige was in her apartment, saying, 'Wait! I live here!' [But as a ploy,] I told the moving company they could either deliver Paige's belongings or pack them right back up and return them to Biddeford. ...Paige was having a fit. She really thought that was what was going to happen," said Cathy.

Paige humorously reacted to Cathy's threat to have her household belongings returned:

I was ready to take my bags home because I knew this lady was crazy. I thought she was going to send all my belongings back to Biddeford! I told her that if my things were going back to Biddeford, I was going with them. At that point, all I needed was the slightest excuse to return to Biddeford. Everything worked out in the end, and we had a good laugh about it later'.

Paige's new job at the State Office Building was exciting during working hours. But in the evening, she found it depressing to go home to a lonely apartment in a rundown neighborhood in an unfamiliar city. It was all she could do to keep from retreating to Biddeford in hopes of recapturing her old job. She missed her roommate, her old friends, and her boss Dick Tryon. But her past experiences with relocating had taught her that it would take time to work through the loneliness and the challenge of meeting new people. As always, she would have to deal with people's initial stereotypes and prejudices based on her appearance. But she made a conscious choice to focus her energies on her new responsibilities at work. She attempted to fill the empty nights with phone calls to friends. She also looked to her ever-present source of support to get her through trying times - God and church.

Love and Loss

Almost immediately after moving to Augusta, Paige began scouting out churches. She attended a local church her first Sunday in Augusta, knowing that it was an essential ingredient for working through difficult life situations. She also decided to keep busy with advocacy activities in the evenings. Every day she prayed that she would make it through this wrenching transition. As always, her prayers were answered. In October, Paige met a man at a self-advocacy meeting who came to occupy a large place in her heart.[1]

She described him as a "wonderful man" who lived in a group home. She explained to me that he had a mild disability that barred him from gainful employment. They quickly became friends. Several evenings a week he visited Paige's apartment, and they would go out together. Loneliness evaporated, and Paige found herself looking forward to his visits. Soon, she found herself thinking about him all the time - day and night.

"What in the world is happening to me? I wonder if I'm in love?" she asked herself.

The couple became almost inseparable, and the following March, they were engaged. It was one of the happiest intervals of Paige's life. "For most of my life something has been missing - a loving relationship with a man," she said. "Now I have met and fallen in love with a wonderful guy."

They started planning their wedding, which was to take place in 1999. Paige had asked Dick Tryon, a former Lutheran minister and now Justice of the Peace/Notary Public, to marry them. Paige was well aware of the profound ramifications of the marital commitment. Also, she knew they had to plan their finances meticulously if they were to purchase their own home and live independently.

1: At Paige's request, his name has not been used here

One night her fiancé called her with discouraging news. That day he had an appointment with his social worker, telling her all about his relationship with Paige and their plans to marry. The social worker's reaction was alarming. She told him that if he were to marry Paige, he would surely lose all of his disability benefits. Because he was completely dependent upon the supplemental income, food stamps, and medical benefits, he could not risk losing them. If he married Paige, her income would be too high for him to qualify for supplemental income or medical benefits. His social worker tried to make him understand the financial implications of his decision to marry. He knew this much - he really couldn't afford to lose his benefits. He was contemplating breaking off the engagement.

Paige was devastated. She was angry at the social worker for trying to control his finances, yet she herself conceded that she wasn't conversant with the effects of marriage on disability benefits. She found it unimaginable that federal regulations would get in the way of their relationship! Questions darkened their future together. What would happen if they got married and Paige died? Would he still qualify for benefits? What if they married in the eyes of the church and God, but not legally? Then could he retain his benefits?

That summer, Paige organized a conference with the office of Social Security and others to address the issues relating to sexuality, marriage, and benefits. The presenter confirmed the social worker's opinions. It was made clear that even if the couple did not get legally married, but were found to be living together, he could lose his supplemental income, medicaid, and food stamps. He simply could not risk losing his financial support. He had never been successful at holding a job, and his future was too uncertain to jeopardize his benefits.

He was beginning to distance himself, and their relationship was beginning to flounder. She was unwilling to compromise her standards about sex and marriage. In turn, he was becoming more and more frustrated in his need for womanly companionship. In the late summer, he asked for his ring back. Paige cried all night...for many nights.

Fortunately, her work as a consumer advocate was highly engaging and rewarding, providing a measure of distraction from the pain of a failed relationship. During the previous ten months, Paige had made five national presentations in Seattle, Columbus, Phoenix, Washington, D.C., and Idaho. In Maine, she was constantly on the go. Traveling with her trusted driver, Dixie, she would zip up to the northern part of the state to visit a group home in Presque Isle, speak at an event in Fort Kent, and return to work in Augusta the next day. The driving alone took ten hours. The next morning, she might head down to Portland to attend another meeting. She made time in her schedule to get to Biddeford and visit old friends and hopefully catch breakfast at Jonsey's or a supper at Bon Apetit. With seemingly endless energy, she was never idle.

Dealing with Pain and Illness

Paige liked to rise early in the morning and go to bed at about 11:30 pm.

"I have so much to do. And, to tell you the truth, I don't know what the future has in store for me," she said, intimating that she was living on borrowed time. When I would call her from Alaska late at night, she didn't seem to mind. Feeling that I might be imposing on her, I asked her when she usually went to bed. She told me not to worry about calling her late at night, because she had to stay up as late as she possibly could in order to maximize the amount of time that she could sleep without being awakened by leg cramps.

"Hey, if I go to sleep before 11:30, I'll never make it through until the morning without leg cramps. Don't worry!" she explained matter-of-factly. It was just one of the many medical problems that she would bear silently.

Paige rarely discussed her pains, dismissing her problems with the knowledge that positive attitudes and beliefs are fundamental to the healing process. When discussing a potentially serious physical problem, such as falling when her legs buckled, or when the doctor told her she needed to use a wheelchair, she would say "Well, we'll just deal with it." The other member of the "we" likely referred to her higher power.

Sometimes Paige's ankles and legs swelled so painfully that she had no choice but to seek medical help. Her doctor recommended a series of tests to determine whether her kidneys were malfunctioning. When I asked her how the tests turned out, she said things would be "okay," and that she was given two alternatives for treatment: either dialysis or a kidney transplant. These two alternatives would be intensely disturbing for anyone to contemplate. In hindsight, I wish there had been more follow-through on her kidney problems. Perhaps dialysis or a transplant would have lengthened her lifespan.

In general, Paige's approach to physical problems was sanguine, consistent with her optimistic outlook. She refused to dwell on disease and relied on prayer for healing. She possessed tremendous faith and put it to work at all times. Focusing on negative outcomes or illness was anathema to Paige. Her positive disposition seemed to have worked, as physicians marveled at her ability to control her diabetes through diet and at her gritty tenacity in walking again after needing a wheelchair for several years. How I admired her ability simply to put negative thoughts and worries aside and turn to fulfilling her goals!

Of course, there were moments when she worried about her physical condition, which she explained in a chapter she wrote for the book *Silver Linings*:

> *I think the most difficult thing for me is all the things that are happening with my legs. Until about four years ago, I could run, jump, and walk just like anyone else, but now I use a cane and wheelchair to get around. I can't climb stairs, which makes it very difficult. The nerves in my knees and legs aren't very strong and sometimes my legs give out on me (Engle, 1997, p.91).*

Paige didn't want anyone to worry about her. She downplayed her physical and medical problems, and when she was forced to rely on assistive devices, such as a wheelchair or crutches, she assumed a light-hearted attitude toward her disability. She painted her wheelchair a shocking pink and referred to it as her "Pink Panther."

"If I'm gonna use a wheelchair, it's going to be fun," she said.

By exercising her faith and engaging in therapy, including therapeutic swimming, she was able to free herself from the wheel chair. She still relied on crutches or a walker, as her legs sometimes gave out completely and unexpectedly. When her doctor told her that she should get shoes that would support her ankles, her solution was to purchase a pair of high top sneakers with blinking lights. The next day she went to work wearing a dress and her flashing high top sneakers. She laughed and jumped up and down to keep the lights blinking.

She found it rough going to transport her beloved Coca Cola while using a walker, spilling her drinks as she was constantly on the move. Using a bit of ingenuity, a friend attached a "sipper" holder to the walker with velcro - perfect for a woman on-the-go.

Muscle spasms in her legs could occur at any time, causing a tight knot and extreme pain until they relaxed. During the spasms, she simply rubbed her legs, never uttering a word. Quiet courage, strength, and humility were among Paige's most admirable and amazing traits. Doubtless, many people never realize how irksome it was for her to maneuver through each painful day. Pain medication was not working, so she relied on her ability to maintain a positive attitude. She said:

> *I have a lot of reasons to keep on going. I want to help others who have had similar difficulties. I've made some very special friends and have come to know the Lord. I can do all things through Christ who strengthens me.*

Irony of Beauty

Paige's work was intrinsically rewarding, and she would have performed it without recognition. However, she loved attention, and it enhanced her advocacy work. In addition to the National Victory Award and her appearances on the *700 Club* and the *Today Show*, she was the subject of numerous newspaper articles and several magazine articles, including those in *Psychology Today* and *Hope Magazine*.

In September, 1995, Nancy Garland, a journalist with the *Bangor Daily News*, who had previously published several newspaper and magazine articles about Paige, wrote a cover story for the Maine Style section entitled "Reclaiming Her Own: Woman Makes Her Mark After Leaving Institution." The essay just happened to appear side-by-side an article about the winner of the Miss Maine Pageant which applauded the local support and community service activities organized for raising funds to support Miss Maine's trip to the Miss America Pageant in Atlantic City, including a chartered "fan bus" for the trip to the South. A picture accompanied each story: one of the gorgeous, bejeweled, Miss Maine and the other of Paige addressing a group of students from The University of Maine. Several weeks later, a poignant, insightful letter to the editor appeared in the paper, written by Kristina Ryberg:

Irony of Beauty

It is not every week that I find such satirical resonance on the cover of Maine Style; however, today while reading your two feature articles on Paige Barton and Miss Maine, I couldn't help feeling the beauty that emanated from the entire page.

On one hand, we have Ms. Barton, who has spent her life overcoming adversity, surviving institutional captivity, and proving her worth as a thinking, intellectual being. On the other hand, we have Miss Maine, who has spent her life battling, competing in, and winning competitions that validate her identity and dream of becoming a representation of women, "educated, talented, and intelligent and health conscious."

Ms. Barton was misdiagnosed with Down's syndrome and was labeled mentally retarded for 36 years and was a first-hand victim of the negative experiences and consequences that label carries. Conversely, Miss Maine has been labeled as "winner" and "beautiful" throughout all of her pageant work since the onset of her dream 19 years ago.

We see Ms. Barton, who has had little support from family and professionals, yet aspired to attain a bachelor's degree, founded a statewide conference for disabled people, and seemingly made a strong commitment to "the ability in disability." On the other hand, we have Miss Maine, who has a fan club of supporters, at home and in Atlantic City, cheering her through the throes of the swimsuit competition and the onslaught of interviews, singing performances, and rehearsals.

Oscar Wilde captures this irony of beauty by stating, 'I have found that all ugly things are made by those who strive to make something beautiful, and that all beautiful things are made by those who strive to make something useful.' As a member of the human race, I wish for men and women the courage, perseverance, strength and beauty of Paige Barton so they can keenly see through the veiled beauty of Miss America.

-Kristina Ryberg, Bucksport
Bangor Daily News, September, 1995

Ryberg's letter to the editor suggests that, as a society, we should review and question our present standards of beauty. Throughout Paige's life, she had been plagued by society's disdain for her external appearance.

People reacted to her as if she were inferior, as if she were not beautiful. Because of this adverse, "gut" response, no one would take her seriously or deem her "normal," whatever that nebulous term means. In October of '98, she was in Wal-Mart buying a pumpkin and a carving knife when the cashier at the check out counter asked her companion if it were "ok" to let Paige have the pumpkin and knife as if Paige's appearance equated with inability to know right from wrong. How tempting it would have been for Paige to tell him that she had a college degree; that she had personally met former First Lady Barbara Bush, actor Christopher Reeves, Maine Governor Angus King, U.S. Senator Bob Dole and Maine Congressman John Baldacci; that she had rubbed shoulders with heads of state agencies, and that she made more money than a cashier, and, ultimately, tell him where to go. But she just smiled and shrugged it off, as she had in similar unpleasant situations for most of her life.

In the late 1980s, I attended an international conference on Down syndrome in England. Surgeons delivered presentations about the controversial procedures for changing the physical appearance of children with Down syndrome through plastic surgery. Slanted eyes could be widened, cheek bones and nose bridges built up, and tongues reduced in size. Actually encountering children who had the plastic surgery as well as seeing many before and after pictures made me doubt the wisdom of these invasive procedures. Was plastic surgery just another example of our society's obsession that everyone look the same? Was it simply equivalent to a rejection of the appearance of people with Down syndrome? Or, does plastic surgery have the potential to truly improve the quality of life for these children, perhaps by reducing tongue size to facilitate speech?

To me, children with Down syndrome are as beautiful as other children, if not more so when they smile. Perhaps I feel that way because
of the many wonderful times and positive relationships I've had with
children and adults who happen to have been born with an extra 21st
chromosome. Stereotyping or making simplistic predictions about
what people with disabilities can or cannot accomplish is, at the minimum, inappropriate and potentially limiting and destructive. I once
heard a young man with Down syndrome play enchanting classical
piano music in a concert hall. I have watched actors and actresses with
Down syndrome on television and in the movies. I have heard pithy
presentations made by eloquent speakers with Down syndrome. I have
also known and loved people with Down syndrome who could not
speak, read, write, or walk - but they all are beautiful in my eyes.

Images of Paige: Savvy Professional and Precocious Teen

At times, Paige was self-possessed and mature beyond her years. At
other times, she seemed immature and uncouth. She enjoyed being a
nonconformist, thumbing her nose at social conventions and wearing
whatever bizarre, or at least unchic, outfit she felt like wearing, and
behaving however she felt like behaving. Sometimes, she was obstinate
and childlike.

Certainly I was more of a conformist than Paige. My sons accused me
of being overly serious, and they were probably right. I was always
working, in one of my professorial roles as a teacher, writer, and consultant. I did most of my writing at home, and my life was a constant
push to meet deadlines. I never had a moment to spare, and my poor
children had to adhere to my tight schedule, whether they had to be
rushed to day care, a soccer game, or to bed. But when Paige was

around, it was difficult to take myself too seriously. Her presence forced me to slow down, and I found reprieve in her outrageous antics. My self-imposed humorless and stressful life welcomed her spontaneous exuberance and enthusiasm.

Nonetheless, there was one thing Paige and I were both very serious about - our work in the disability field. Paige always had a cheerful smile, and she knew how to maintain a sense of humor and how to be playful. In contrast, I was less adept at maintaining the delicate balance between work and play.

Paige's good friends Peggy and Steve Cantrell insightfully described the facets of Paige's personality in their *SOFT Times* (November/December 1999, p.10) tribute:

> *There were two distinct people residing in Paige, the child who had been robbed out of her childhood and the adult who could be articulate, bright and mature, but Paige really didn't like that role - she preferred to be the precocious teenager.*

Pam Healey, the Massachusetts and Maine SOFT Chapter Chairperson expressed a similar observation, characterizing Paige as:

> *...at once the child now adult with the chromosomal diagnosis, with her own vulnerabilities, and the professional who understood the vulnerabilities of others...She carried the old life with her as she met new challenges and in turn freed others. It was the two layers of Paige that were important, that combined to form her vision of herself and others, that determined the way in which*

she envisioned and acted upon the possibilities." (Soft
Times, November/ December 1999, p.7)

The stories recounted by Paige's colleagues and Maine's self-advocates
reveal her layered, dual-sided personality. Dennis Strout, Support
Person for Speaking Up for Us in the greater Portland area, interviewed
Paige's friends and several self-advocates in early summer 2000. In
meetings with consumers in three regions of Maine, he taped their stories. The delightful anecdotes captured impressions of Paige as a savvy
pioneering professional as well as a playful, precocious, sometimes rebellious youth. She was an articulate advocate for people with disabilities, serving as their voice and their champion. She was also a person
with a disability, a Maine self-advocate, and a self-declared sibling to
children with Trisomy 18 and 13.

Dixie Leavitt remembered first meeting Paige at the Kennebec Valley
Assembly of God Church in 1996, when she overheard Paige telling
Pastor Puckett that she needed a driver to do her work. At the time,
Dixie needed the extra work and made a bid for the job. She started
driving Paige to her professional meetings and visits to self-advocates
throughout the state, beginning in late April.

Paige was a very meticulous person, and she wanted things done right
and on time, said Dixie.

> *I went to work for Paige in April, and I didn't get*
> *my first paycheck until July first. And she was just*
> *having a hissie fit! I kept saying: It's OK, Paige. Just*
> *think of what a big check I'm going to get! And when*
> *I got the check, she asked, 'Did you get a big check?'*

> *I said yes, and she said. 'Good. Take me for an ice*
> *cream!'*

Paige's supervisor at the Office of Consumer Affairs, Cathy Bustin Baker recalls several images of Paige. Her first encounter with Paige was at a mental health conference discussion about eight years before they worked together.

> *There was still a debate about whether people with*
> *mental illness could live outside of institutions. I*
> *was sitting in the front, and all of a sudden from*
> *behind me there was this big booming voice. I turned*
> *around, and there was this woman that I had not*
> *met before who was talking about Pineland Center's*
> *closing, and stressed that people with disabilities cer-*
> *tainly could live in the community and how she was*
> *a living example. I thought, 'Oh wow, I need to meet*
> *this woman!'*

Another image Cathy recalls was seeing Paige in her wheelchair, rush-ing to a legislative hearing in the State Office Building, beeping a horn to clear the path ahead. One day, unbeknownst to Paige, she was beep-ing her horn behind Governor Angus King.

One of Cathy's final images of Paige was of her in the hospital before her death.

> *They were taking blood gasses from Paige, and it*
> *was very painful...We tried to get her to think about*
> *something else, so we encouraged her to sing her trol-*
> *ley song. That was Paige, characteristically turning*

pain and frustration into humor.

Friend and self-advocate Vanessa Munsay and supervisor Dick Tryon elucidate one of the most well known stories about Paige at the first Consumer Conference at the Sheraton Hotel in South Portland, which Paige called "The Beer Can" because of its tall, cylindrical shape. Paige's ability to coordinate a conference for over 300 people, many with bulky wheelchairs, attests to her impressive organizational skills. The week prior to the conference, she and Dick went to the Sheraton to prepare the staff for the conference. They tried to educate them about the conference participants - to apprise them of ways to antici- pate the needs of people who relied on assistive technology, or to know what to expect from those who had visual impairments, or to be alert to the possibility that someone might, unpredictably, jump into the pool. The two also met with the hotel security people to be sure every- one was oriented properly. Dick related the incident as follows:

> *The first night after the Marcia Rosen Award ceremo-*
> *ny, Paige wanted to throw a party for the awardees.*
> *She asked me if she could use my room for the party*
> *because her roommate was going straight to bed. I*
> *said yes, so after the dance she went on up to my room*
> *with some friends. About an hour later I headed up*
> *to the room. I'd just stepped inside the door to find*
> *everyone laughing. Next I saw security guards in the*
> *room. 'We've had a report that someone was jumping*
> *up and down on the floor of this room, and we have*
> *to check it out,' they said.*
>
> *That was the only time that the conference plan-*

ners or hotel security had any problems! With Paige's
jumping up and down on the bed because she was
so happy about the success of the conference! Un-
fortunately, she annoyed the people in the room
downstairs, and they called security. It was the only
problem, but it happened in my room, of course. So
at every conference from then on, Paige had to have a
"bed jumping" party in her room.

Fellow church member and self-advocate Maryann Preble simply described Paige as "funny." Maryann, a former resident and survivor of the Pineland Center (institution) and another self-advocate, 24 year-old Chandra, liked to sing the "Trolley Song" that Paige wrote:

Trolley Song

Oh by gosh by golly
See the little red trolley
And it makes me very jolly
To ride on the little red trolley
And the trolley goes ding ding ding.

The two women laughingly related that they always sing this song when they see the trolley in Augusta. The words to the song, along with Paige's name, are now posted inside the trolley car. A flyer about the trolley was distributed in Augusta, complete with Paige's song. Chandra has a fond memory of a song Paige created about Zoloft, an antidepressent medication Paige had been prescribed to quell her worry and anxiety. She questioned why she was taking Zoloft, and expressed her complaints about how it affected her in a song.

The Zoloft Song

Silly silly silly
I'm so silly silly silly
I'm so silly silly silly . . . do you care?
Silly silly silly
I'm so silly silly silly
I'm so silly silly silly . . . do you care?
Zoloft makes me silly
And it makes me really flakey
And I feel like I'm in outer space somewhere
Silly silly silly,
I'm so silly silly silly . . do you care?

Paige's immature streak most likely originated in her being shut away, missing the socialization with a diversity of peers. Moreover, her ebullience stemmed in part from her feeling like a bird out of a cage, emancipated from the gray imprisonment of institutional life. However, several scholars have observed that some of our greatest leaders and thinkers, like President Franklin D. Roosevelt, Winston Churchill, Mark Twain, and even Einstein possessed an adolescent streak, as Paige did. Paige resembled them in her readiness to defy perceived and thus often obsolete wisdom, her high-spirits, and her can-do attitude, all of which at times seemed shocking to people who Sinclair Lewis termed in *Arrowsmith* as stuffy "Men of Measured Merriment."

Chandra narrated the funny tale of the time when she and Paige were on their way to a self-determination conference in Philadelphia. When they boarded the plane, the attendant apologized to all the passengers for delaying the flight "because of time it takes for the people with disabilities to board the plane." Boarding the plane into the Pittsburgh airport was an ordeal because the gate turned out to be wheelchair inaccessible. Two men, looking backwards and facing away from the steps, manually carried Paige from the airport to the plane. Chandra was afraid that Paige would "fall right out of her chair" because of the dangerous tilt and positioning of her apparatus.

Chandra confessed that she herself has a dangerous habit of "taking off," or bolting, when she becomes anxious. One day she "took off" from Hallowell, ending up in Paige's office located at the Augusta Mental Health Institute about four and a half miles away. "It turns out that everyone was looking for me," she said. Thereupon, Paige gave her some highly useful advice about dealing with her anxiety attacks. Paige taught her that whenever she was anxious to repeat the incantation to *"Stay Cool, Stay Calm, and Stay Collected."* Even now, Chandra finds herself repeating these words almost like a mantra, when she encounters difficult situations.

Chandra especially liked accompanying Paige and the Kennebec Self-Advocacy group to Funtown, an amusement park in Saco, and savored the memory of her friends screaming with delight as they rode the huge roller coaster, fearsomely nicknamed Excalibur.

On her own, Paige had a passion for amusement parks, and recounted to Dixie anecdotes about day trips to amusement parks when she was institutionalized. She told of how the residents were taken as a group to the park, and told by the staff exactly which rides they were allowed to take. At Funtown, she caught herself asking Dixie for permission to go on a particular ride. Dixie gently reminded her, "You're not in an institution anymore. You can choose your own ride." When Paige discovered that she could ride on the roller coaster as many times as she wanted, she exercised her freedom by riding it again and again.

Paige believed in the principles of normalization and natural proportions. A large group of people with disabilities descending on a community facility, whether it be an amusement park, a movie theater, a church, or a restaurant, creates a spectacle of the consumers and can place an extra burden on the facility's employees. When the proportion of people with disabilities is too high, their opportunities for independence and typical social interactions with nondisabled people who are not caregivers are minimized.

Paige was also wary of segregated group activities that had overtones of charity, such as Special Olympics. Ideally, she believed, people with disabilities should be able to blend into community activities that reflect an individual's personal choices and preferences and that provide the requisite adaptations to make participation possible.

On the other hand, the "strength in numbers" of people with disabilities in self-advocacy organizations, such as Speaking Up for Us or People First, was an entirely different matter. Paige maintained that people with disabilities themselves must fight for their rights and exercise self-determination by banding together. She believed that progress could not be achieved effectively by paid employees or nondisabled people alone. It could not be accomplished by a single person or only a few. To affect obligatory changes in services and public policies, collective action was imperative.

Paige's good friend from Bangor, Carmella Stackhouse, who attended self-determination conferences in Toronto, Boston, and Albany with

Paige, mused on Paige's personal magnetism and her legacy. When asked the question "What attracted everyone to Paige?' she responded, "Her story...how she survived...and how she would advocate for others. Paige would tell us: "You can do it! Speak up for yourself!"

"If it weren't for folks like Paige, do you think people would accept us?" said Carmie. "You can't learn from a book about the person that's disabled. You can only learn it from us - from our stories."

Carmie displayed the valuable knowledge she acquired at the conferences and from Paige: "Paige helped me be a stronger person; she helped me stand up to opposition better. I remember one very stressful Speaking Up for Us board meeting. We thought Paige was being driven out of the organization. We got upset and a lot of us walked out. Including me."

When Paige went to work for the state as a Consumer Advocate, many self-advocates believed it was inappropriate for her to continue as a leader in the self-advocacy movement. The self-advocates decided to change the name of "Speaking for Ourselves" to "Speaking Up for Us," because they felt that the original name was tied too closely to Paige and Community Partners, Inc. Dick Tryon remembers how difficult it was for Paige to back away from her involvement with Speaking Up for Us. "This was an important time for the self-advocates to become more independent, although it was a painful period for Paige," he said.

Carmie explained her distress about the future of Speaking Up for Us and the Consumer Advocate position Paige held with the Department.

"Are they going to hire someone else in that job who hasn't walked a mile in our shoes?" she questioned. "Could any of us qualify? I want to apply for that job, but I don't have the typing skills and I don't have a college degree." Carmie was also uneasy about the future of the annual Speaking Up for Us conference. "The conference should carry on her [Paige's] name. Paige loved every one of us. She always urged us to "Pass the Torch."

Paige was effective in her job because she had walked a mile, and then some, in her consumers' shoes. She elucidated this point in the Community Partners Booklet:

> *I have my own apartment. It is with the support that I get from CPI that I am able to be as independent as I am. I get bills and pay them promptly. Sometimes I wake up in the middle of the night worrying about being on time for my appointments. I laugh and I cry just like you.*

> *But because I do have a disability, I'm different. I know what it feels like to experience prejudice. People with disabilities are usually feared, misunderstood, and ignored. I feel this is because we represent something that society sees as imperfect, flawed, different in some way, and sometimes an embarrassment. I think that's where prejudice comes from. Actually we are just like everybody else. We want to look nice, be successful, and be accepted in society as human beings. We want to be appealing and to be special.*

In other words, Paige was declaring that many people fear those who seem to act in idiosyncratic ways or who deviate from socially accepted norms - in actuality, impossible-to-attain stereotypes - and make them invisible or deem them pariahs.

Paige's own chronicle of disability placed her in a unique position to serve the noble purpose of creating more caring and inclusive communities. She did so through helping people with disabilities speak for themselves. As an employee first of Community Partners and then of the Department of Mental Health, Mental Retardation, and Substance Abuse, she was charged with advocating for, and standing behind, consumers of mental retardation services. Because she grew up as a person considered to be disabled, she had been a consumer herself and could empathize with others with disabilities. At times, she wasn't successful at maintaining her professional role as an advocate and would slip into a consumer role. For example, she was reputed to be too assertive in her capacity as a conference organizer, and needed to allow others to make the key planning decisions.

As a Consumer Advocate, Paige found it imperative to control her own inclinations and empower her constituents. She knew they needed to make their own decisions and choices. However, letting go could impede progress because she couldn't always depend on others to follow through on their well-meant promises and good intentions. As an advocate, she would have to curtail gradually her assistance as the consumers made strides in engaging their own talents in living and working in the community.

Promoting consumer choice and self-determination was Paige's greatest professional priority.

Paige's impact as a consumer advocate for the Department of Mental Health, Mental Retardation, and Substance Abuse was demonstrated by a dedication ceremony held at the AMHI Complex the year after she died. Convened by Lynn Duby, Commissioner of DMHMRSAS, the program included remarks by those who knew Paige, ending with a speech by Maine Representative Randall L. Berry who was sponsor of the following Legislative Sentiment that now appears on a plaque in the Office of Consumer Affairs. The plaque was designed by Robert Wing, owner of American Awards in Augusta, who wanted to assure that Paige's courageousness and tenacious beliefs were not forgotten.

In Memory
PAIGE BARTON
Office of Consumer Affairs
DMHMRSAS

Through her mentoring, support and
encouragement of people with disabilities,
Paige helped people focus on their "abilities"
and through her tenacity, sense of humor and
fun loving spirit, advocated for others and
helped them to "Speak Up For Themselves"

Epilogue

I Shall Be Released

The idea for this life story was inspired by a friendship between two women who shared a very special bond and common life purpose. Both journeyed through a period in history when American society was grappling with the proper treatment and education of people with disabilities. As adolescents, we both walked the halls of some of our nation's largest institutions, witnessing the horrors inside. But we were on different sides of the door, one locked within and the other free to go.

In the early 1970s, when I was a graduate student at West Virginia University, I toured institutions for persons with mental retardation in Pennsylvania, West Virginia, and Ohio. Later, when I was an adjunct instructor for David and Elkins College in West Virginia, college students in my special education classes accompanied me to observe the deplorable conditions and absence of educational services in these institutions. At the same time, Paige Barton was in Ohio at the Apple Creek State Hospital, and later the Lake County Mental Retardation Center, living the experience. I observed only as a spectator.

In 1975, while I struggled to move the students of the segregated "Trainable Retarded Youth Center" into a public elementary school in Elkins, West Virginia, Paige was simply existing in a segregated residential facility. Her link to the world outside the institution was solely through her work with young children with severe disabilities in a nursing home. At that time each of us had, independently, concluded that the key to future success in life - both for ourselves and for people with disabilities - was to be educated and to help educate others. We were both determined to accomplish something that was going to require discipline, sacrifice, and plain hard work. While Paige tried to convince her caretakers that she could take and pass the GED exam and obtain her high school equivalency diploma, I was applying to the doctoral program in educational psychology/special education at the University of Minnesota.

Our lives intersected in a most unlikely place - the University of Maine at Farmington. This book reflects a deep and ongoing friendship, which continued over thirteen years, often at a distance when I moved to Montana and Alaska, and when Paige moved to Biddeford. Yet we always kept in touch through phone calls and letters. In the summer of 1996, the Today Show was catalytic in physically reuniting us in Maine. When I returned to Maine to work at the university in Presque Isle, we had lived apart for 7 years. For the Today Show, Sofia Faskiamos and her crew filmed Paige for over 13 hours. I was honored by being identified as Paige's mentor and friend. The film crew drove from Biddeford to Presque Isle, sharing several days with us complete with a special roadside visit by a moose and a delectable lobster feast in Caribou.

Return to Apple Creek Institution

In 1997, Paige and I had a unique opportunity to revisit a dark segment from her past. She had been invited to be one of the keynote presenters, along with actor Christopher Reeve, for the "Abilities in

Motion: Solidarity '97 Conference," in Columbus, Ohio, on May 30th. Paige told David Zwyer, now Executive Director of the Ohio Developmental Disabilities Council, that she had been a resident at Apple Creek and was ready to go back for a brief visit and face up to that period of her past which was so dismal and painful. He arranged for both of us to visit Apple Creek State Hospital on the second day of the conference.

I had been invited as Paige's support person for the conference. My function was to accompany Paige, assist her with travel, especially boarding airplanes, and to room with her at the Hyatt Regency in Columbus. I was actually looking forward to being her support person - to my relief, I wouldn't have to plan a presentation or give a workshop. Being a university administrator had been so exhausting that I relished the thought of being in the background for a change. It would be a golden opportunity to complete the research for the book we had contemplated for years. I was cautious not to raise my hopes too high, because so many years had transpired since Paige had resided in the institution. In fact, I seriously doubted that they would even have Paige's records.

On June 1st, we arranged for a rental car and visited Apple Creek State Hospital, now called The Apple Creek Developmental Center. It was pouring rain, and the sky was very dark and ominous. Despite the rain, I could see that the countryside and green rolling hills of Wayne County's Amish country were beautiful. Our drive from Columbus took about 2 hours, providing ample time to turn Paige's anticipation about the visit into anxiety - then raw fear. I wasn't sure she would be willing to step foot inside the doors of the institution. She confessed to me that she had nightmares in the hotel room about being held captive in the institution. Repeatedly, I assured her that no one would ever allow that sort of bondage to recur. Juxtaposed to her fears was her desire to heal wounds that were buried deeply in her past and that lingered in her heart.

When we arrived at the little village of Apple Creek, we stopped at a drive-in restaurant for a quick lunch. I ordered a burger, fries, and a soda, but Paige was too nervous to eat. I coaxed her into having a drink, so she ordered her usual Coca Cola. But she barely touched it.

It wasn't easy to find the entrance, and we drove right by it more than twice, cruising the Ohio countryside. Perhaps the sign was obscure or perhaps it was because the institution's name had been changed from a state hospital to the Apple Creek Developmental Center. The new name, we found out later, accompanied a change in institutional purpose and size. When Paige lived there, the population was 2,500, whereas in 1997, the population was only 210. Now there are less than 2100 individuals in the entire state of Ohio served by the Ohio Developmental Centers.

At the time of our visit, Apple Creek housed adults ranging from age 22 to 75, and although it was still a residential center, it had a new vocational training component. In contrast to past practices, residents were encouraged to live semi-independently, doing as much of their own cooking, laundry, and personal care as possible. Great effort had been made to create a more homelike atmosphere, including training in leisure skills.

Knowing that we were coming, Superintendent Michael Snow had gathered a welcoming committee for Paige. A number of the women who had known Paige - most retired, one the former Directors of the Patient Aide Program - had rearranged their day in order to greet this former resident and friend. They rolled out the proverbial red carpet, greeting Paige with warm embraces.

Initially, we went to the snack bar where Paige was presented with a precious photo of her as a Patient Aide. After some reminiscing, Mr. Snow arranged a tour of the institution, replete with an entourage that included the Operations Director and the staff members who had known Paige.

Paige had asked to see the building in which she had resided. As if the weather weren't menacing enough, our walk through Macintosh Hall had the makings of a hit horror film. The foreboding brick building had been closed several weeks before our visit, and the electric lights weren't working. Mr. Snow had a flashlight, so we could see the eerily lit hallways. The rooms still contained the same rickety old furniture, which was about to be auctioned off.

As a group, we walked the haunted halls of the first floor and then went upstairs. Paige was insistent that I see all the places she had told me about. I felt remorseful for doubting her stories about Apple Creek. Everything, yes everything, was as she had described it. We saw the upper porch where Paige had fallen while running. We saw the room where she had been punished with solitary confinement, complete with a small barred window situated in the heavy door - as if she were in jail. But most disturbing was the treatment room where Paige claimed to have received the dreaded electroconvulsive "therapy." She pointed out exactly where the operating table was, and although the table was gone, we could still see the electrical sockets for the wiring that delivered the massive, often debilitating doses of electricity.

We entered the large room where the patient aides diapered and fed the young children. When we stood in the large dayroom that overlooked the semi-circular tree-lined driveway in front of Macintosh, Paige paused for several minutes to gaze quietly out the window. She told us that she used to wait there on weekends and look out in hopes of seeing a visitor. More often than not, she said, "no one came," and her loneliness persisted, unabated.

After the tour we returned to the administration building and Super-intendent Snow asked how he might help us. We were both amazed at the amount of time he devoted to Paige's visit. He invited us to sit in a nicely remodeled conference room and asked whether we wanted to review Paige's records. A member of the welcoming committee who remembered Paige was in charge of the institutional records. She had found Paige's entire file, which was almost two decades old. Simultane-ously Paige and I looked at one another. We were both stunned and elated.

For years, Paige and I had talked about writing her story. I was ashamed at how I had procrastinated. In the meantime I had edited two editions of one book and had authored another. Somehow I could not embark on Paige's book. The real reason, which I had not fully revealed to Paige, was that there wasn't enough information and documentation for me to piece her life together. Yes, there might be a magazine article, but an entire book? I thought not.

I also had misgivings about writing about her institution experiences when I had no proof. Was she really drugged as she said? Was she re-

ally placed in solitary confinement? Had they really administered electroconvulsive shock treatments to patients? Mr. Snow walked in with
a yellowed file about three inches thick. As we sat in the conference
room reading, now riveted, from the institution records, I was speech-
less, astounded. Right there in the medical reports - in black and white
-- was the date and dosage level for the Thorazine!

In the file was a picture of Paige on the day she was admitted. "Wow,"
I said. "This looks like a prison 'mug shot!'" But I was almost moved
to tears when I saw the innocent smiling face of the youngster behind
the name plate. Indeed, it was a mug shot - no different from those
photos routinely taken of incarcerated prisoners. I could have read the
records all night long, but by then it was almost 5:00 p.m. We had
monopolized almost the entire day of the Superintendent and his staff.
He asked Paige whether we wanted photocopies of some of her records,
and we eagerly agreed. At that moment, I made an oath to myself to
finish the book.

Paige was treated like a dignitary at Apple Creek. It was heartening to
witness the change in attitudes that has occurred over the years. The
gracious Superintendent and his staff were extremely sensitive to Paige's
pain over her past institutionalization. As recompense, they welcomed
her with warmth and kindness.

Abilities in Motion

As we drove back to Columbus, we shared our amazement at what had
happened that day and what we had seen. After an elegant dinner at
the Hyatt Regency, we returned to the hotel room, falling into an exhausted sleep. Both of us knew that Paige had to focus on her keynote

presentation for the next day.

The Solidarity '97, "Abilities in Motion" conference was attended by several thousand Ohioans with disabilities, many using wheelchairs and other assistive devices such as electronic communication boards. On the first day of the conference, actor Christopher Reeve was the luncheon keynote presenter. Reeve, an actor, particularly famed for having played the lead role in the popular Superman movies, ironically was paralyzed from a fall while horseback riding. Since his accident, which made him a quadraplegic, he has turned to movie directing and serving as a spokesperson for people with disabilities.

Reeve's message was as touching as it was powerful. The most poignant and controversial aspect of his presentation was his use of the word "cure" as a possibility for people with spinal cord injuries. At present, when the spinal cord is severed, it does not repair itself, resulting in irreversible paralysis. Reeve campaigned for greater funding for research to find therapies and even complete cures. He rightly believes that recent breakthroughs in research on the repair of spinal cord injuries are a harbinger of future healing and restoration. His message was one of hope as well as of courage. There was no self-pity evident in his speech or his demeanor.

Reeve was absolutely correct in stressing the importance of federal research dollars directed toward medical research and rehabilitation. Without scientific and medical research, his vision, and the dreams of thousands of people with spinal cord injuries will not stand much chance of realization. His dream is not limited to spinal cord injuries, but physical disabilities and mental disabilities as well. His rationale was that if we can explore other planets, we can find cures for many disabling medical and neurological conditions.

Paige's keynote on Friday morning was also a message of hope and courage. She shared her life story in an objective, factual way, tracing the steps from living with her family to her institutional placements and her determined progress through the university where she obtained her degrees.

Although Paige's life story was always fascinating to audiences, what they seemed to appreciate most was how she has managed to reach her dreams despite the Trisomy 18 - mosaic, despite years of institutional- ization, despite the lack of encouragement, despite her chronic medical problems. Paige's message was one of determination - believing in one- self and in God. She dared to dream, and she dared to fail. When she had behaved in ways she was not proud of, or when her behavior didn't serve a higher purpose, she tried to abandon that behavior. She also had a remarkable ability to let go of the past, to forgive others who had hurt her, and to focus on actualizing her dreams for the future.

I never knew Paige to indulge in self-pity. Yes, like most people, she felt pain and emotional hurt, but she met them with fortitude and for- giveness. She has somehow managed to forgive the profound mistakes of others that resulted in years of her life robbed by institutionalization. She was not bitter; instead, she was willing to try to understand why she was mistreated.

Paige also refused to fret about things she could not control, such as her health. She tried to adhere to a healthy lifestyle, and refused to indulge herself in the many aches, pains, and medical problems she ex- perienced. She refused to succumb to a wheelchair until she absolutely could not walk. When her lungs were so filled with fluid that she could hardly breathe, she took herself to the hospital to have them suctioned. When her legs were swollen with fluid from malfunctioning kidneys, she promised to watch her diet and do whatever it took to avoid dialysis or a kidney transplant. Paige possessed a faith that helped her relinquish worries about her health and the future. She replaced agonizing with self-reminders of her life's purpose. She openly expressed gratitude for the many blessings she has been given, particularly for her friends, her family, her education, her life's work, and, most of all, for God's love.

Paige radiated the light and assurance that accompany a strong religious faith. Fundamental to her faith were prayer and forgiveness. Her unwavering belief in God saw her though many troubling times and inspired her to follow through on her dreams, even when no one believed she could accomplish them. How could she pursue her goals with such vigor in the shadow of everyone's skepticism?

It is possible that the challenges and seemingly insurmountable barriers Paige faced were each cornerstones in building her character. She had an unrelenting determination and commitment to reach her goals. There is no doubt that her life challenges contributed to building her character. She was highly successful at transforming negative experiences into positive ones. Whether we initially fail or succeed is not the point - what's important is discovering that persistence pays off.

Paige also attributed her determination, and her "stubborness," to qualities that she inherited from her mother. Her goals of obtaining a college degree were also consistent with her family's esteem for higher education.

When one asked Paige what she valued most, her answer was straight-forward; she valued each day she was alive and able to work and be with her friends. Like many people with disabilities or serious illnesses, Paige did not take her life for granted. Rather, she filled her days advocating for people with disabilities. Even the week before she grew fatally ill, she spent every day of her vacation taking her self-advocate friends to lunch and to ride on the little red trolley.

Ryan Cantrell's Annual Balloon Release

The annual Support Organization For Trisomy 18 and Related Disorders (SOFT) Balloon Release was very important to Paige. It gave her an opportunity to remember her departed loved ones. She released balloons for her sister and for her father. Her prayers also went out to her departed SOFT siblings. Balloons are the symbol SOFT uses for children who have made the transition to their heavenly home.

Because Paige had a very tender, emotional side to her personality, she felt safe in freely expressing her feelings and her tears at the Balloon Launch. The event was sorrowful for her, because each year so many children with Trisomy 18 and 13 passed away.

Losing innocent children and infants to a chromosomal disorder is heart breaking - an agony very difficult to accept. Inevitably, questions arise in the minds of parents and family members. Why does my child have this disorder? Why did God take our little angel? The answers often remain hidden, but many parents have found support and consolation in the understanding and caring members of the SOFT organization.

Peggy and Steve Cantrell of St. Louis, Missouri, established the first SOFT Balloon Release in honor of their son Ryan. On October 4, 1985, Ryan was born with Trisomy 18. Shortly after his birth, he was rushed to Children's Hospital, fighting for his life. He returned home after two weeks, but his time at home was interrupted with a dizzying roller coaster of hospitalizations. On Christmas Eve, he was struggling to breathe because of pneumonia, and after the church service was rushed by ambulance to the hospital.

Steve and Peggy said:

> *Ryan faced an uphill battle through near death episodes, ending up with a tracheotomy and ventilator. We were able to take him home in March. At this time there weren't any pediatric ventilators with battery back up so we were required to hook up a large house generator just in case the power failed.*
>
> *With twenty-four-hour nursing and converting a bedroom into an Intensive Care Unit, we actually had some wonderful family time and were able to bond with our son. We had a birthday cake and balloons once a week and condensed a lifetime into his short life. Looking back, it was the best!*
>
> *Early Sunday morning, June 15, Father's Day, Ryan's alarms went off and the nurse shouted for us to come quickly. We knew something was very wrong, and she began CPR. He was taken by helicopter back to Children's where they worked on him for 3 hours . . . but it was just his time. The nurses were his nightime Moms and Dads,*

and they really gave his life-or-death condition their best effort. We were very touched by all of this extra effort.

Ryan's short life had changed ours forever - he did not leave us where he found us! We decided to turn his funeral into a celebration and a tribute to his short life. We surrounded him with his favorite toys and lots of helium balloons. We gave each friend a balloon to take to the cemetery. It was a clear day with blue skies and a little breezy. The balloons chattered to each other as they tried to get away. Our pastor used to use the words of Jesus as He had told Lazurus's friends to "Unbind him and let him go." With that everyone released their balloons and they were off, traveling Heavenward together. We were transfixed and somehow the ritual made us feel better.

Three months later, over the Labor Day weekend, Peggy and I were jogging in the woods near our home feeling totally depressed and despondent. As we approached our driveway, there on a limb was draped a blue balloon with a tag hanging from a string. The tag read: "God Loves You."

We felt this missive was hand delivered and somewhere out there someone knew we needed a lift. We shared this story at the very first SOFT convention in Salt Lake City, and soon after began the balloon release as a celebration and tribute to our children. This has become an annual tradition ever since and has a healing effect on new families.

Paige's Balloon Release

The first week of August 2000, Dixie Leavitt and I were able to attend the SOFT Conference in Orlando, Florida. Dixie created an album of pictures and memories of Paige to display in the "Memory Room" at the conference, a room that had been designated for reflection and remembrance of the children who had passed away.

I was particularly interested in attending the tribute to Paige scheduled for one of the noon luncheons. It was an impressive session with speeches by Dixie, Pat Farmer, and Kris Holladay plus a video of Paige on the Today Show. The conference provided me with a wonderful opportunity to meet and interview many of the people Paige had talked about over the years. I met a woman from Australia, Tracy Pass, who claimed that "Paige gave the best hugs!" Tracy was selected as the person to take Paige's "Hope Bear" to Australia for young Alex, who has Trisomy 18. The Hope Bear was a teddy bear that was placed on Paige's computer at work by an unknown person the week preceding her death.

I could see why Paige loved this organization. A sense of community and warmth pervaded the atmosphere. The SOFT children were clearly the focus of the conference, and they were fully included - warmly embraced - in the meetings and events. They appeared to be thoroughly enjoying their Disney experience!

Dixie and I were planning to attend the Balloon Release on the last day of the conference, and I confess that I was a bit uncomfortable about going, not knowing what to expect. Busses lined up at the Coronado Resort to transport families to Camp Ithiel for the ceremony and barbecue picnic. We rode for what seemed like a very long time to a wooded park area. The sky was darkening as threatening clouds moved in. I was disappointed because the weather had been so sunny for the entire conference. Maybe, I grumbled to myself, if we hadn't driven so far to get to Ithiel Park, the Balloon Release would have taken place in the sun! It was early evening, and I was tired, hungry, and grumpy.

The busses pulled into the park, and everyone headed to the lodge. Unloading the children from the busses could have been an ordeal, but it was conducted gracefully. The parents didn't complain or seem to mind the effort, not to mention grousing about the strength required to carry their children, the wheelchairs or strollers, the diaper bags, and other paraphernalia. Their serenity and cheerfulness quickly changed my mood.

As we all made our way toward the dining area of the lodge, it started to rain lightly. In the lodge were several tanks of helium to fill the colorful balloons. Before the conference, those who wanted to set free a balloon in memory of a child could request a balloon using the registration form. Both Dixie and I had made our requests in advance, so at the conference registration table, we received beautiful white paper bags with gold lettering. Inside the bag was a blue booklet of poems with a colorful rainbow on the cover called "Soft Words of Comfort," a tiny white angel made of white fabric, pearls, and delicate lace; a pad of paper inscribed "Remembering our Angels;" and the printed tags to attach the balloon strings. Printed on my tag was the Angel's name: Paige Barton, Birthdate: 10/25/51, and the Angel Date, 8/24/99.

The ceremony was about to begin, and Peggy Cantrell, using a microphone, requested that everyone sending a balloon aloft gather in a ring next to the lake, which was down a short incline beneath the lodge. The raindrops were giving way to sunlight, as the sun lowered in the west, shimmering through the clouds and illuminating the trees and the navy blue eastern sky. The music to the song "Somewhere Out There" sounded in the air, bringing tears to my eyes because it was a melody Paige and I jointly performed using sign language for one of her speeches in the eighties.

It was a beautiful, tranquil spot, with an opening in the trees to allow for the thirty-five balloons to rise unobstructed. Parents and families gathered together, balloons in hand and tears streaming down the cheeks of many.

Dixie and I found a spot on the periphery of the circle. She instructed me, "When they call Paige's name, let your balloon go." Unexpectedly, the red balloon left her hand. "Oh, no! I can't believe it! It's too soon!"

Dixie was clearly disappointed about prematurely releasing the balloon, when a man came over to her and said, "Don't worry, the exact same thing happened to Paige's balloon last year. It got loose before they started calling the names."

"Maybe Paige would have appreciated the repeat performance," I tried to console Dixie. Peggy started calling off the list of names. When I heard Paige's name, I raised my hand up and let go of the string. The balloon floated into a nearby tree, catching on a large limb. It was the only balloon that became tangled in the trees.

As we looked up, a beautiful rainbow suddenly formed in the eastern sky. A chorus of "Ahhhs" conveyed the sense of wonder among the people in the ring. The rainbow symbol appears throughout the SOFT literature. The timing of the rainbow was impeccable.

Something made me turn to Dixie and say, "I predict Paige's balloon will wait for all the others, and then when the last one has gone, hers will extricate itself from the tree so it can shepherd the rest to heaven." As we got to the end of the alphabet and the last name was called, sure enough, the balloon started migrating to the end of the branch. It was about to be freed from the branch, when a man came over and shook the tree. Precisely at the moment after the last balloon was launched, Paige's yellow balloon left, wafting skyward.

As we walked back up the hill from the ceremony, an old friend of Paige's, Mike Healy, came over to Dixie and said, "You won't believe this, but in the middle of the Balloon Release ceremony, my pager started beeping. I pulled it out of my pocket to check the message, and guess what it said?" Dixie couldn't guess. "It said I had a message from Paige Barton, Office of Consumer Affairs, and that she was in Florida at the SOFT Conference and would return the e-mail when she returned."

In the morning, Mike had tried to e-mail Dixie, who was now using Paige's old computer in the Office of Consumer Affairs. For some reason, the electronic response confirming the receipt of his e-mail occurred hours later during the Balloon Release, setting off his beeper. "You can call it coincidence, but I know better than that!" Indeed, the timing was impeccable.

I will always remember the beautiful rainbow and the two balloons, one that took off prematurely, as Paige's balloon had the year before, and the other which was trapped in the tree branch until the rest had been released. It was a sign. Yes, it was time to unbind her and let her go, I thought. It seemed that Paige wanted us to know that she was with us in spirit and that everything was all right. Walking up the hill from the lakeside to the lodge, I saw a bright green bromeliad growing on a loose piece of bark lying on the ground. I picked it up as a memento of the beautiful ceremony. This "air plant," or epiphyte, grows without soil, gaining its nutrients from the air and moisture, growing on other plants for support and structure. Like the bog plants in the moxie water in northern Maine, and like Paige Barton, they flourish in the sparse nutrients in their environment. Both display a beauty of substance, that unexpected endurance which is tempered by adversity in the harshest of situations. How fitting a memento of Paige Barton.

Paige's mission of helping others to speak for themselves should move forward. Her dream was for individuals with disabilities to reach their full potential and make their own choices. Many of Paige's talks ended with a sign language performance of the song "Touch Through Me." In expressive silence, with only graceful, fluent hands, Paige conveyed how the Lord worked through her to help others. Paige knew that every one of us is capable of touching and blessing others' lives, no matter our situation or disability.

References

Barton, P. (1997). A retreat from asylum: Finding my place in the real world. In S. Engle (Ed.), Silver Linings: Triumphs of the chronically ill and physically challenged (pp. 85-96). Amherst, NY: Prometheus Books.

Blatt, B. (1981). In and out of mental retardation: Essays on educability, disability, and human policy. Baltimore, MD: University Park Press.

Blatt, B. & Kaplan, F. (1966). Christmas in Purgatory: A photographic essay on mental retardation. Boston, MA: Allyn & Bacon.

Evans, D.P. (1983). The lives of mentally retarded people. Boulder, CO: Westview Press.

Frank, L.R. (Ed.). (1978). The history of shock treatment. Self-published, San Francisco.

Goffman, I. (1961). Asylums. Garden City, NY: Anchor Books.

Lakin, K.C. & Bruininks, R.H. (1985). Strategies for achieving community integration of developmentally disabled citizens. Baltimore: Paul H. Brookes.

Nirje, F. (1976). The normalization principle. In R.B. Kugel & A. Shearer (Eds.), Changing patterns in residential services for the mentally retarded (rev. ed). Washington, DC: U.S. Government Printing Office.

Stenson, C.M., Daley, S.E., Holladay, K., Farmer, P. (1999). Trisomy 18: A handbook for families. Omaha, NE: Munroe-Meyer Institute, University Affiliated Program, University of Nebraska.

Stevens, L. (2000). Psychiatry's electroconvulsive shock treatment: A crime against humanity. Retrieved March 5, 2003, from http://www.antipsychiatry.org

Szasz, T. S. (1970). Ideology and insanity: Essays on the psychiatric dehumanization of man. New York: Anchor Books, Doubleday & Company, Inc.

Support Organization for Trisomy 18, 13, and related disorders. (1999, November/December), The SOFT Times, 1-13.